The author grew up in a lower middle-class section of Brooklyn. She went to 12 years of Catholic school. Barely 18, she got married and moved to Long Island. Her two brothers joined the service at 18. She had always been a quiet child but always appeared disheveled. There was nothing feminine about her in her early years. She always looked sad. One day she had a dream and everything about her changed.

Dedication

To God – I would not be here if it were not for Him.
To my children – who were there when I wasn't.
To Dianne – who inspired me to put my life on paper.
To all the lost souls out there who believe they have no hope.

Patricia Jolls

HE CALLED ME AHAB

AUSTIN MACAULEY PUBLISHERS™

LONDON • CAMBRIDGE • NEW YORK • SHARJAH

A CIP catalogue record for this title is available from the British Library.

ISBN 9781788482639 (Paperback)
ISBN 9781788482646 (Hardback)
ISBN 9781528954303 (ePub e-book)

www.austinmacauley.com

First Published (2019)
Austin Macauley Publishers Ltd
25 Canada Square
Canary Wharf
London
E14 5LQ

Acknowledgments

I would like to take time to thank my daughter Christine, who advised me, when she was told that I was writing a book, to not think of it as a book but just writing my feelings down. That took a lot of the pressure off.

I would like to thank my daughter Linda and my son, Joe, who have supported me emotionally throughout this process.

I would also like to thank Dianne who, upon receiving a few pages of this book at a time, showed interest in my words, which made me continue writing.

I would like to thank most of all the editors of this book and the wonderful publisher who took a chance on an unknown author.

I think we can all agree that when a baby is born into this world, he or she is innocent and pure. They are emotionally undamaged at this point—kind of like having blank pages in a book. This story is about one such child who was born in 1946. That child is me. I changed some of the names as my family is still around and I don't want them embarrassed.

The mother of this child was a dreamer—one who lived in a world of her own imagination. She was a princess, a dancer, a pleaser who took on the guilt of the world. All of these things of her own making. She was the baby of four siblings—one boy who was the oldest and three girls. They were children of an Irish couple who came to New York from Ireland.

I can see her even now, dancing around the living room in a flowing dress to the sound of the Glenn Miller Band. It didn't matter who was there; she wasn't aware of anything but the music. She became the music—drifting, flowing as if she were a soft wind in the early spring. Grace in the purest form.

Watching her, I really wasn't thinking about how she was in the 'after being sober and before being drunk' mode. She was just this person in her own zone and it made me feel happy, if only for a moment, until the reality of it all hit. And it usually hit hard. She would be either falling over drunk or something would click in her mind and she would be instantly fighting with her husband—inevitably, something would always happen. The change would happen right before my eyes. Suddenly everything would be different. The mood was different—the air stopped, the music stopped. The kids ran and that pain in the pit of my stomach came back. Everyone knew 'someone' was in trouble; the kids became invisible again.

The girl knew instinctively that she was the strongest of the three of them, having two brothers. So if anyone was called by the parents, she was the one to show up. She felt the need to protect her brothers. But this was okay as she was strong enough to handle it. The 'it' could have been anything—from making them a Manhattan to taking the blame for something—getting them a beer or helping one of them off the floor. But she could do it. By the age of ten, she could even make dinner for the family and had to do just that many times. And soon, the parents became dependent on her for their dinners, so come Friday night, she knew she would have to make dinner as this was the beginning of their weekend.

I didn't realize it at the time but I learned a lot from these experiences. It does feel good to be in your own 'zone' but just not using any substances to get you there. I became very protective of that zone and kept it to myself by not allowing anyone to see where I was or what I was thinking. And being invisible is great because you can be anyone you want since nobody sees you. But I didn't really experience the freedom that it gave me until years and years later. The inner strength that was being developed also didn't show up until much later in life—at least I didn't notice it until later. Other people may have noticed it, even mentioned it to me, but I had never believed compliments.

Anyway, getting back to the parents. The father—he had no 'zone' of his own. He had a flat effect most of the time as he hid his feelings, if he had any. He was very quiet when he was sober. I actually never heard a normal conversation between the two parents like how their day was at work. But, when the father had more than two drinks, HE SPOKE. Sarcasm is the first thing that comes to mind when I think of him now. Degrading someone was what I see now as his lifetime goal, and I believe that I was his only target. But after five drinks—that's when the rage came out. And if it didn't by that time, passing out was next, after a few more.

He was an only child of a quiet English banker gentleman whose words I can only remember were to me. "If there were

10

nothing on the floor, you would find something to trip on," as I tripped over his brown shiny shoe. So I was clumsy. Still am. I never saw him in anything but a suit, white shirt and tie—just like his son.

His wife, who was my grandmother, was a pure German woman. She was kind and always did the proper thing but couldn't drink more than one alcohol drink without becoming giddy. And I bring that up because drinking had been a great part of my childhood.

But neither one of them ever 'saw' me. Although I found out years later that she was watching me but never spoke up. Grandma was a great cook; the family went there every Sunday for dinner for a period of five years. With all those Sunday dinners, you'd think I would've developed some feelings for my grandparents—good or bad—but I didn't. It was just a place to get some good food and the parents wouldn't get too drunk, so it was tolerable.

You know, thinking back on this childhood, I don't remember one instance when I even liked the father.

Growing up, there was a feeling of either 'us' or 'them'; there was no true feeling of family. It's easy for me to look back and say this but at the time, I really didn't know what 'family' was supposed to feel like. I remember an incident when I was 14 years old that is hard to forget. I don't remember how it started, but I see myself on the porch of a house we had rented. I was standing on that porch watching the upstairs neighbor fighting with my father—fist fighting— and he was on top of my father punching him. I felt a rush of anger and reacted instantly as I pushed past my mother and brothers who were standing in the doorway and went into the house, and got the biggest carving knife I could find. Putting it to the neighbor's throat, I screamed (with spit coming out of my mouth), "Get off my father or I will kill you." Oh, he got up—FAST. I believe I would've done it if he hadn't listened. The next thing about that night I remember was the family sitting in the living room and the police knocking on the door. The officer spoke calmly and stated what just happened, looked at me and said, "He said it was your daughter that had the knife."

My reaction was that of shock. "Me?" I said very innocently. "He said I had a knife?" The reality of that response was totally believed by the cop.

He apologized and left, but did say, "No more fights." We moved within a week. How could someone who hated their father so much risk death or going to jail to protect them? I was confused at this point.

I think the biggest unsolved memory with the father happened when I was about ten years old. They were fighting again—throwing bottles and glasses and whatever else they could put in their hands. I was in my room under my blanket, pulling it over my head, and I remember humming so as not to hear the yelling and the smashing of the glass on the walls. Then, SILENCE. I stopped humming. I heard the father's voice say, "I'm going to take the only person in this house who understands me." I believe my teeth were chattering by that time. *Please not me, don't let it be me,* I thought. "Patty," that's what he called me, "get dressed; you're coming with me." My ten years of life with the parents taught me to never talk back or question anyone—EVER.

So, I got up, dressed, and went with him. He brought me to the St. George Hotel in Brooklyn. It had a huge pool in the lower level and the bar overlooked it. They had rental bathing suits there so my father told me to go get a bathing suit and get in the pool, which I did. There was no one else in the pool and it was cold. I remember looking up at the bar and he was standing there staring at me with a drink in his hand. I was shivering at that point and just stood there. You would think that going to a swimming pool would be a good experience for a ten-year-old, but it was far from that—I felt scared and alone.

What I remember next was walking into the hotel room and seeing only one bed—which was the first thing that I noticed. I slid under the cover on my left side holding the side of the bed with my right hand. I slowly turned around and looked over my shoulder. I saw him sitting at this round wooden table drinking his Manhattan, I would guess. The next thing I remember was waking up and feeling his right arm around me as he said, "Oh, Nan,"—which was my mother's name (Nancy). I FROZE.

After that I remember I was walking about ten feet behind him on the sidewalk. No matter how hard I try to remember more, I just can't. And that's all I remember about that.

But I never thought of my childhood as being bad or unbearable. It just was what it was. But I carried around my secret (about my parents), their drinking and bizarre behavior, and as a result, became very quiet. I was (looking back) a loner—in the true sense of the word. I got ignored at school and if anyone did talk to me I would hear, "What you talking to her for?" I went to a Catholic elementary school and during playtime they would make us play games. I hated it. I was never picked for anything and if it were dodge ball, I was STILL invisible. They didn't even try to hit me with the ball— 'maybe they were afraid of me'? Well, I did do some out-of-character things. I remember once following this girl home; she was the most popular girl in the class. She was smart, pretty, and wanted to become a nun. Every time she turned around I would hide. She finally saw me and began to run home crying, "Why are you doing this?" she cried. I had no idea why I followed her. I did this to another girl, too. I know they never deserved it and I don't even know why I did it. Maybe I wanted to be seen or feel powerful—who knows?

I never liked school and never studied. I couldn't concentrate enough and I felt like all that they were trying to teach us wasn't important anyway. I considered myself plain and felt ugly. I never looked like, or felt like, I belonged. It was just me and I didn't even count for anything. It sounds like I felt sorry for myself but I didn't; it's just the way it was.

The first time I had sex was when I was 14 years old. He was 20—and by far not the best looking. I met him through my older brother (he was a year older than me). Let's call my brother Tom. Well, Tom was still in high school and began hanging out after school at this luncheonette called the Embassy. It was owned by this old frail man who was called

'Jimmy the Greek'. I remember him always walking from behind the counter with a broom in his hand saying, "Time to sweep up—you got to go—time to sweep up." He did that to chase everyone out of the luncheonette. I can't say that I blamed him—nobody ever bought anything—they just used his booths to hang out in after school. My brother came home one day and told me about this guy he met at the Embassy where he hangs out. "You should see his muscles," he said. I could see that my brother looked up to him, so one day after high school I met my brother at 'Jimmy the Greek's' luncheonette to meet this muscle guy. There were about six or seven people there and my brother introduced me as "this is my sister". I pulled up a chair as there was no room in the booth. I sat there, never saying a word. Then this old man, probably in his 40s, got up to leave and said to me, "I'm pleased to meet you, young lady," and kissed my hand. WHAT??? He saw me and even treated me like a person. Later my brother asked me what I thought of 'Steve'. I thought he was talking about the owner of the luncheonette but soon realized that he was talking about the man who kissed my hand. My first thought was *ugly* and *old* but since my brother looked up to him so much I didn't answer him. I began going to the Embassy every day after school and got to know the other people as well as Steve.

After seeing Steve with the crowd almost every day after school, I began feeling more comfortable around him. About three months later he took me to a nearby park and before I knew it he had his pickle in me. He even pushed my head, my face on it, and I cried. That was disgusting and wasn't even fun at all. That whole thing made me feel dirtier than I was. Just another secret to keep. Just thinking about it makes me want to vomit and this is the person I ended up marrying as I cried going down the church aisle. Who was I? How could I have done that—I didn't even like him! But I guess I figured I always dreamed of being a mother and this was one way to do that. And I guess, at the time, it would've been better than living with the parents.

I was 18 at the time I got married and my older brother, Tom, had joined the Navy. He had come home on leave to be the best man in the wedding.

At a young age I recognized that I had a lot of anger but didn't know why at the time. It didn't help that my older brother bullied me. One day Tom talked me into standing in the doorway of our apartment at the age of ten and pull my panties down and bend down so that two of our boy neighbors could see my butt while my brother collected 15 cents from each of them. I hated that I did that and it turned out to be one of the many things that he held over my head. "I'll tell them (the parents) about what you did with those boys," he would say whenever he wanted me to do something for him. He even used to sing their names to torment me. And torment me, he did. There were a few other things he made me participate in, which I regretted.

I lived on Ocean Avenue at the time in Brooklyn. That was actually the longest period of time (five years) that we ever lived in the same place. One day as I was walking around the corner I saw this lady who had five puppies in a box that she was giving away. There was this one puppy who was very quiet and sitting in the corner of the box shivering. He was the only one who was all white and I picked him up. The lady said, "You can keep him." I fell in love with this little puppy. That night, I put some towels in my toy box and put him in it before the parents got home. When they did get home, I told him to be quiet and shut the top of the toy box. But the puppy had other ideas though and began whimpering. As much as I begged him to stop, it didn't matter. I heard, "What is that noise?" as the parents stood at my doorway. In a split second, my brother was standing at the doorway saying, "She did it. I didn't know about it." I begged my parents to let me keep this poor puppy who had no home now. After many promises to feed him, walk him, and take care of him, they said, "Yes." I couldn't believe it. My own puppy. Right on my bed he went to spend the night with me.

The next day my aunt Florence—who was my grandmother's sister—brought me a collar and leash. She died of breast cancer a few years later. I was probably nine years old at the time.

One day as I was walking 'Duke', as I named my dog, I noticed a man I had seen before, walking with some groceries. He was very overweight and breathing very heavily. I asked him if I could help him. He handed me the packages as he thanked me. He was grateful as he lived about a block away. After I gave him the packages at the basement door of his building, he said, "I forgot to pick up bread. Would you be able to get the bread and bring it back?" As he handed me the money. I remember feeling uneasy but knew he couldn't make it back to the store so I said okay. So Duke and I ran to the store which was probably about a block and a half away and ran back. I got to the basement door and yelled, "Hello!" It was so dark in there but I heard him call, "Bring it back here." I saw a light, way at the other end of the basement. I felt scared and kind of sick as I was walking through this dingy, dark basement all the way back to the lit room. There he was, sitting in a big swivel chair, and next to him was his large brown boxer on a leash. All I heard was his very heavy breathing as he said, "Come over here." I walked over to him, very slowly, fully aware of how scared I was but really wasn't sure if I should be scared or not. *I'm not a baby,* I thought. I handed him the bag and he said, "Keep the change and here's a brand new Spalding ball for you." I was so impressed with the ball, as I had never owned one of my own. So, I put it in my pocket and handed him the bag. Immediately after taking the bag, he said, "Come over here and sit on my lap," as he put the bag on a table. I didn't want to but I also didn't want to get into trouble if I didn't do what he told me, so I sat on his lap. He put his hands on my chest and rubbed very hard back and forth as he asked, "Does this feel good?" The blood rushed out of my face and I jumped up and ran out of there so fast that I pulled the collar right off of Duke—and ran all the way home so fast that my own dog couldn't keep up with me. Duke followed. My heart was racing and I felt like I didn't care about anything. I went up the three steps on my stoop and threw the money and the ball down. I didn't want any part of them. I felt sick and scared—things were racing through my mind—I didn't know if this man would tell my parents what I did—did anyone else notice? I felt like I was in very big trouble. I stayed inside for the rest of the day with racing thoughts of what would happen when the parents got home. They didn't say anything about what I went through so I didn't tell them anything about it. I was even paranoid at that young age that I would think that they knew what happened. Years later I heard the man died of cancer, and I had no feelings about that one way or another. It just was.

Anyway, not long after that encounter—BOOM—it happened again. The parents used to take us kids to Coney Island or Brighton beach every Saturday or Sunday. I vividly remember this one day. I was wading in about three feet of water over my waist when someone pinched my vagina (hard). My first thought was that it was Tom, my older brother. But then I thought, *I don't think he would go that far*. I followed this figure, with my eyes, as he was swimming away under water. At that point I didn't know if it was an animal or a person but I was determined to know who did that to me. About ten seconds later this older man, maybe 40, balding and heavy, emerged from the water about 25 feet away and just looked at me. I honestly didn't even have an urge to call the father, having no clue what he would do, so I just got out of the water and set out to find my parents. These beaches were packed, with each blanket practically touching the next one. I never said a word about what happened. It was just another secret. I never felt like I had enough information about the parents or their reactions to be able to depend on them to support me or to talk to them about very devastating events in my life. I felt dirty that day and embarrassed. Again I felt like I was in BIG trouble—in the pit of my stomach.

The only male, up to this point, that hadn't hurt me was my baby brother Christopher. He was four-and-a-half years younger than me. I adored this child. I felt like Christopher was my child, as I protected him from the parents. I treated him with kid gloves and didn't want anything to harm him.

You know, looking back at these instances in my life, they seem so trivial now but I believed they shaped my life. I'm still a loner and have never had someone I could trust enough to get close to emotionally. I'm really not sad about that; it's just the way it is. Oh, maybe I get lonely once in a while but it passes fast. I'm okay.

My father stood about 6'5", wore glasses, very skinny, and had black thin hair which was always parted on the left side. I never remember him laughing or even smiling and could never tell what he would do next. My mother was 5'5", slightly overweight, and had short lighter brown wavy hair. She looked Irish. She smiled and laughed especially when she would have a few drinks. I don't remember either of them hugging me or saying 'I love you' EVER. It was like living with a married couple who were strangers. I do remember my mother talking to her sister one night when she stayed over, who was my aunt Kay, and saying, "But she's so tall." My feelings weren't hurt by that; I had no feelings about it at all. I knew I was tall for my age—still am tall.

My father was constantly correcting me. He corrected the way I walked, my teeth (which has a space between the top front teeth), the way I looked and wore my clothing, and the way I talked. When I say correct, I really mean 'made fun of'. I could not do or say anything without my father saying something about it. It got to the point that I just wouldn't say anything. I remember when I was 22-years-old and came over to visit with my parents. I already had my first child Linda, who was about two years old. We were in the living room and my father told me to "come over here and sit on my lap". I hesitated, thinking, *Don't you think I'm a little too old for that?* But would never say that out loud. "Come on over here—what do you think I'll do—get a hard-on?" Even with him saying that, I sheepishly went over there and sat on his lap. *Ewww*, I remember thinking—*this is disgusting.*

Another time when I was 13 years old and it was early in the morning, still in the Ocean Avenue apartment, I heard some screaming. I woke up and couldn't see. I put my hand in front of my face and wasn't able to see it at all. Everything was black. I couldn't breathe so I made my way over to the window, opened it, and took a deep breath. I could see the black smoke pouring out of the window. I heard my mother's voice so I felt my way to the bedroom door which led to the hallway and grabbed hold of someone. As I passed the dining room and the living room, I could see the fire on the walls, ceiling, couch and table. Those rooms were clear of smoke for some odd reason. I heard the crackling of the fire and was just amazed at all of it. Someone pulled me to the front door. The front door knob had melted so it took a few minutes to get out. As soon as I got out and the door closed, I cried for Duke and told my father to open the door so I could get him out, but he couldn't. Tom and I ran across the street and pulled the fire alarm. I looked across the street and could see the flames coming out the windows but all I cared about was Duke. I remember looking at Christopher as his skin was so white and clean and ours was black and dirty from the smoke. I could actually taste the smoke in my mouth. Christopher actually walked below the smoke line in the apartment and never got all the soot on him like we did. The fire trucks came and I pleaded to the first fireman who went into the building, "My dog. Please get my dog."

By this time everyone was out of their apartment and in the courtyard. I could hear them making plans to have us stay somewhere for the night. I waited and waited, watching the door to the building. Out walked the fireman carrying my dog. I felt devastated. "No, Duke!" I screamed, but then I noticed him move.

"I found him with his nose stuck in a brown shoe," said the fireman. He was alive! They later discovered that a lit cigarette in the sofa started the fire. That was the second fire I was exposed to.

The first one happened on Lawrence Avenue in Brooklyn when I was about five years old. We lived on the second floor over a shoemaker. From what I can remember, the shoemaker was very mean. I must've been four or five years old and my brother and I would play in front of the building. The shoemaker would come running out with a belt in his hand screaming, "You kids are ruining my business playing in front of the store." We would run away from him but never told the parents. I felt sorry for the man and assumed he was poor but was puzzled, as I didn't remember him having any business at all for us to ruin.

But back to the fire. We woke up to a lot of screaming and laughing as we looked down the hallway and saw the hassock on fire and my father beating the flames with his suit jacket. They yelled for us to get away and go back to sleep as they were laughing. I couldn't go to sleep for hours until I saw that there was no more fire. We never knew how that started. My father said it just got too hot out and it started to burn. But knowing that the parents both smoked cigarettes, I knew it had something to do with that.

My earliest memory of my childhood is when we picked up my baby brother Christopher Joseph from the hospital a few days after his birth. I was sitting in the backseat of a car my father was driving. I begged my mother to let me hold him (Christopher). She put him in my arms; he was so tiny and pure. When I looked down at this beautiful, tiny baby, I swore then that no one would ever hurt 'my baby brother'. I wasn't going to allow him to go through what I had gone through. I remember thinking, *I would be his protector.*

In chronological order my next memory was when I was six years old. I remember that I was sitting on the rug in the hallway of a hotel in Atlantic City with a man standing over me asking what I was doing there. I didn't know. I didn't feel good and I felt very confused. All of a sudden, the elevator opened and my parents were standing there. I later heard, about three days later, that I had a fever of 103°. I do remember hallucinating that there was a man in the hotel room looking around. At least that's what my parents told me, that it was a hallucination. We probably stayed there for five to seven days until I got better. I guess we were on a trip of some sort because our next stop was in South Carolina. Our parents never told us what was going on—just took us along. We stayed in a motel, on a hill, and must've been there for a while because my brother Tom went to a kids' birthday party. So we were there long enough to know somebody.

After that we lived in a house in Augusta, Georgia. The parents got us a dog that we named Dusty. He was a beautiful Cocker Spaniel with light, golden-brown hair and every time he wagged his tail, it dusted the floor. Hence, the name Dusty. My parents must've worked and my brother and I went to school there. I don't remember the school at all, but what I do remember is coming home with my brother and a couple of other kids and trying to show off by jumping on the sofa in the living room. The next thing I saw were stars and heard the sound of my hair being ripped out. It was the maid. She pulled me across the room by my hair as she was screaming at me. Somehow, I guess my parents found out because there was a different maid the next day. Of course, I never told them. One day Dusty got out of the house and ran for the highway, which was not far from us. I followed him. It was just dusk but I could see the bright lights of the car coming, and knew that he would chase the car when it passed as he had done that before. Just as Dusty was crossing the highway to chase the car, another car came out of nowhere going in the opposite direction and ran him over. All I heard was 'Thud! Thud!'. I couldn't believe my eyes as I ran to him and put him in my arms and cried with him. I heard my brothers' voice in the background, "Get out of the street; there are cars coming!" he screamed. I just sat there with Dusty. I didn't care about anything else. I believe my brother went back to the house and got the maid who took Dusty and me home. Dusty went to 'sleep' that night. I knew what that meant but was not too sad about it since Dusty had been whimpering in pain for a few hours. I can't tell you how long we lived there but I do know that our next stop was on Windburn drive in Atlanta.

I was seven years old at the time. This was a large two-story house setback maybe 200 feet from the street and we lived on the second floor. It was Christmas time and I remember my brother getting a BB rifle for Christmas. Tom told me he wanted to try it out so we went across the street to a small wooded area. There he told me to take off my left shoe and sock. I always listened to him even then. I didn't want to get into any trouble, so off came my left shoe and sock. He told me that it wouldn't hurt and I believed him, and before I knew it, he pumped the rifle up and pulled the trigger. It hit me an inch from my little toe and 'WHOA' did that hurt. I began to cry but he told me not to be a baby or he 'would tell'. I still carry a slight indent as a reminder. You know, it had never even entered my mind that he was the one who did something wrong and not me. So, I stopped crying. It was after that the thumb incident happened. My brother found this can—like a tuna fish can—that still had the handle with the thin metal rolled up on it in the backyard. I was told later that it was a key that they used to open up the can. The tool came with the can as there were no can openers at the time, I guess. While my brother unrolled this strip of metal and told me to hold onto the strip very near the key, he said, "Hold on tight and watch this." As I held on to the metal, he pulled the key very fast and all I heard was the metal scraping against my thumb bone. Then came the pain. There was blood everywhere. He gave me a story to tell the parents so he wouldn't get into trouble and I really didn't want him to get into trouble; after all, 'the damage' had been done already, was my brother's reasoning. I never did that again though.

Mind you, I'm only saying things that I remember. I mean, I know I went to school there but don't remember anything about that. My next memory is that of a washing machine out in the back yard in the same house. It had these two rollers on top of it that were used to wring out the clothes. My brother got this idea that I should put my right hand between the rollers to see if I can separate them. Well, I did, and he turned on the switch and the rollers pulled my hand and part of my lower arm in and I began to scream until one of us turned it off. I can't tell you how much that hurt. Tom yelled at me for being 'so stupid' and got my parents to get my arm out. Of course, I never told my parents what really happened, as I just thought it was another stupid thing that I got myself into.

I'm not sure how long we lived there but I do remember being in the St. Patrick's Day parade. Maybe I was in it through school. I don't know why but being in the parade made me feel important—like I counted for something. On my birthday, which was three days earlier, I got a blue bicycle which I rode for the first time in the driveway the day I got it. So after the parade, I took my bike and rode it up the hill on the other side of the small forest across from the house, which in reality was probably an isle with trees. Coming down the hill was thrilling to me—the speed, the wind—a sense of freedom until I got to the curb of the isle and quickly realized that I never learned how to turn. So, BAM, I hit the curb—the handlebars turned as I hit the ground and struck me in the right side as I landed on my left hip. This hurt so bad that I didn't even have the strength to cry. I had to be helped off the ground by my downstairs teenage neighbor and her friend. They practically carried me up the stairs. I could barely move; I was so weak. I begged my brother not to tell my parents since I knew they would take my bike away but he did anyway. A little later, after my parents got home from work, my mother helped me to get in the bathtub. The water was so warm that it made the pain go away for a moment. I remember that when I looked down after I sat in the tub, I saw blood slowly coming out from somewhere. I called my mother. The very next thing I remember was being wheeled on a bed away from my mother and then falling asleep. The handlebar had split my kidney. I still don't know what they did in the operating room but I was told by a nurse that I was a lucky girl. Well I didn't feel so lucky. I was in a wheelchair and stayed in the hospital for about 12 days.

My next memory takes me to Miami near Christmas time. I remember that Christmas Eve, looking out the hotel window we were staying at and swearing I heard Santa's sleigh bell. It felt almost magical or holy to me. That Christmas morning, I woke up to the best present of a baby doll and a cowgirl suit. Tom got a cowboy suit and a truck. In the afternoon that Christmas day, we went out to eat lunch. When we returned to the hotel, we went up in the elevator to the room and for some reason the key didn't fit. When we went down to the hotel lobby, my mother kept us kids away from the desk where my father went. I knew he was arguing with the man behind the desk. When my father came back to us, he said, "Come on, let's go." I told him I wanted to get my baby before we left and he said, "No, they're keeping all the Christmas presents, let's get out of here." My unsubstantiated guess was that they didn't pay for the room. We all spent that night at the Miami bus depot. They didn't have any money for tickets, so we had to wait until they got money from my grandparents. I don't remember how long that stay was. I don't remember the trip back to Brooklyn but I do know I was still seven years old at the time. Our first apartment there, after the trip, was the one on Ocean Avenue, the one I talked about earlier. I think this was the first time I realized that my grandparents were subsidizing my parents' income.

My mother always worked and my father worked sporadically. She was a secretary and my father a bookkeeper. I later found out that my father had stolen some money from a company he worked for and hence the long trip down south. My grandfather was a banker and found out about the theft at a bank Christmas party when someone came up to him and said, "I'm so sorry to hear about your son," and went on to tell him what his son did.

So I'm guessing the grandparents got us the Ocean Avenue apartment, paid for the Catholic schooling, bought us most of our presents, and sent us on all our summer vacations to New England and upstate New York. I do have some good memories of our vacations. My older brother and I were allowed to explore wherever we wanted to—and that we did. There was no harm done during those trips. They were real vacations.

So it was living on Ocean Avenue when I first realized that the parents were alcoholics. They were drunk by 10 PM every night, and sometimes what I call 'roaring drunk' and other times 'falling asleep drunk' or 'tripping drunk'. Right after dinner at 6 PM, sometimes we would put on a 'play' for the parents. I remember that most of the plays were funny or at least they were funny to me. I don't think anyone else got it but I remember that I did. The parents didn't laugh. It was probably me 'acting out' which was not realized at the time. I was the one who organized them and told my brothers what to wear and what to say. This was serious stuff to me.

But growing up in Brooklyn was very educational and rather fun. I took the subway to Manhattan or Coney Island for only \$.15. We had no issues with race or religion when we were growing up. People were people.

So now, after the big fire, we went to live in my Aunt Florence's apartment on Flatbush Avenue. She was staying at her son's home in New Jersey and was dying of breast cancer. By this time I was 14 and my brother 15 and Chris was 10. Tom and I were going to Catholic Prep School and Christopher to Holy Innocents from where we had graduated. The thing I remember most about living there was some 'hush-hush' talk about my brother Tom going to a doctor as he was not 'developing properly'. I kind of knew what that meant. Tom must've been embarrassed, since I saw he got mad whenever they discussed it. Both my brothers were still wetting their beds at that time. Tom stopped the day he went into the Navy and Chris stopped about the age of 13. Well, we stayed in Aunt Florence's until she died—about two to three months.

Our next stop was Linden Boulevard. That's the place I attacked the upstairs neighbor with a knife and is also the place where I met a boy I fell in love with—Rich. I met him one day as I was walking around the neighborhood which I did by myself frequently. He was 16 years old, had blue eyes, and thick dirty blonde hair. He was built well, stood 6'2" and was the sweetest person I had ever known. I would babysit for his sister just to feel closer to him. He lived with his mother and had a job in the city as an elevator operator. I was 14 and it was the first time I spent New Year's Eve at Times Square. Of course the parents thought I was sleeping over a friends' house from school. Rich invited me to meet him there so I talked this girl into coming with me and telling her parents that she would be sleeping at my house. We gave them the wrong phone numbers just in case they did call. Well, we got there and met Rich and his friends. I was always shy, so we walked behind them about 20 feet. There were wall-to-wall people there, so we roamed about two blocks outside the crowd. The girl I was with met two sailors who wanted us to go with them. She wanted to go with them and tried to talk me into going but my heart was for Rich. She left and I continued to follow Rich by myself. By now Rich and his friends were about a half a city block ahead of me. A fight broke out and I saw that Rich got hurt, so I got a little closer and followed Rich and his friends to the hospital. I was the last one in the door and I saw that Rich was bleeding from his head. The nurse took him through the doors. I felt very angry and maybe confused. The security guard asked me what I was doing there. I lashed out at him and said, "I'm here for Rich—that's what I'm doing here. What's it to you?"

He was very kind to me and said, "Do your parents know where you are?"

With that, I cowered and sheepishly said, "No." He asked me how long it would take me to get home and I answered in a very low tone, "An hour."

"What is your phone number?" he asked. I gave it to him. I was so scared that I gave him the right number. He told me to go home and that he would call in one hour. I left crying and crying all the way home. I crawled through the front porch window and sat in the dining room next to the phone until 4 AM. He never called. Now I couldn't stay there since I told my parents I was sleeping at my friend's house so I crawled back out the window and went to Rich's house. He lived on the third floor of a walk-up about 15 blocks away. I sat just a few stairs up from his door, intending to wait for him—for about an hour. His neighbor came home and without even asking me why I was there invited me to come in and take a nap on her couch. At first I said "no" and thanked her but before long I found myself knocking at her door and asking if I could use her couch. I must've woken up at about 10 AM, thanked my savior of the night, and went home. I never did get to see Rich. He did call me a few days later and I met him somewhere; he gave me a ride in his car and asked me out on a date. For some odd reason I chose to go to the St. George Hotel's pool for the date. We went to the pool and I found out that Rich was just as shy as I was. But that night, I believe I fell in love for the first time. We never even kissed. When Rich walked me home, Tom was there in front of the house. He came right up to us and said, "I'm telling." Tom later told me that Rich really didn't like me and I was too ugly for him—how could he? It wasn't long after that when Tom introduced me to Steve. I talked to Rich once after that night and we planned to go to Coney Island after meeting at Rich's sister's house but I never showed up. Maybe Tom was right and I didn't deserve him.

After everything my brother Tom had done to me, I still looked up to him and wanted to please him. Truthfully, I'm not sure why I didn't meet Rich that day. Did I really believe he didn't like me or was I too ugly for him? Or was it because I knew that Tom looked up to Steve and if I could be his girlfriend I would make Tom happy? This turned out to be one of those life-changing decisions for me. I still think about Rich and have even tried to find him, although I don't know what I'd do if I did. Maybe just knowing that he's all right would be enough.

There was one more incident that took place in the Linden Boulevard house. I was 14 at the time. Tom called my name as I slept and I woke up to him standing over me holding his hard penis in his left hand as he said, "Touch it." I pulled the covers over my head and went back to sleep. Neither one of us ever talked about that night.

So, after that horrible night with Steve in the park, I guess we both just assumed that we were 'going out'. Mostly we went with a group to the beach, parties, the drive-in, and out to eat. I remember one party in particular that was in the basement of our house on Linden Boulevard. My brother Tom, as we ran in the same crowd, told everyone he could hypnotize me. This was spontaneous on his part—I think. Of course I wanted everyone to believe Tom, so I went along— he said some words to me and I pretended to be under his hypnosis. He then told me to hold my right arm out and went on to say, "She will feel no pain when I put the cigarette out on her,"—we all smoked at that age. I couldn't believe he said that, but I didn't move. I smelled my flesh as he put his cigarette out on the back of my right hand but I didn't flinch. Everyone was amazed at his ability but that wasn't enough for him so he told me to put my left hand out and then did the same thing to that hand. I didn't want it to go on so I pretended to wake up slowly. Someone asked if I felt any pain. I contended that I didn't and actually looked surprised to see the two burn marks on my hands. I still have those scars to this day. Another secret to keep.

During that time on Linden Boulevard I ran away from home. Some girl in my school named Kathy told me she was going to run away and go to California. She asked me to go with her. I was in the second year of high school and a real mess. I had cut school maybe 20 or 30 days in a row and the school had called one afternoon before my parents got home and told me to tell my parents to call them. I called Kathy and told her I wanted to go with her. She told me she wasn't going to leave until the next Saturday, which was three days later. Well, I had to do something. I wasn't going to let the school talk to my parents so I 'ran away', although I didn't go far. My parents always got home at 6 o'clock in the evening so I would leave the house before they got home and come back after 11 o'clock, use the side door, and sit in this tiny room in the basement under the stairs on a chair with a blanket wrapped around me. It wasn't very comfortable and I really didn't sleep, but after the parents left in the morning, I would go upstairs to my bed and take a nap. That's when I ate and changed my clothes. One night I was walking around in Park Slope after taking a bus there and met this boy who asked me where I lived. I don't know why, but I told this boy that I ran away from home. He was so nice and talked me into letting him call my parents. I took the bus home, walked in the house, and went to bed. They didn't say anything that night or ever. I felt like a juvenile delinquent, a criminal, the 'black sheep', the 'ignore her and maybe she'll go away person'. It was as if it never even happened—it was never talked about.

I was probably 14 near 15 years old when we finally had our own home. Every time we moved, I always thought things would be different now, but they never changed and yet I never gave up hope. Tom was still wetting his bed but Chris had stopped by that time. Looking back at that, I don't know why Chris stopped sooner than Tom. Almost every time my father got 'roaring drunk' he would always say to Christopher, "You're not my son." Poor Christopher. We kids never talked about our feelings to each other but we all knew we loved each other. It had always been 'us' and 'them'.

By this time I hated the father and felt sorry for the mother. I became proficient at cooking and it became my job on Fridays. My favorite was rarebit—easy to cook and clean up. And by the time the parents had their third drink, I was out of the house. They never knew or found out. By this time I was seeing Steve regularly and slowly separated from Tom. I got a job at 16 years old at Woolworths. I had been babysitting regularly for three people but I wanted a 'real' job. My big mistake was telling Tom where I worked and when I got paid. He showed up, without fail, every payday. He would leave me five dollars and take the rest. He always had a sob story to tell me. He knew just how to get to me. By the time he was almost 17 he had left home and was sharing a room with a couple of guys. I realized I didn't even know who Tom was at that time. He enlisted in the Navy at 17 and was gone before I knew it.

I graduated high school at 17 with a scholarship to Brooklyn College and three job offers. I had taken the Civil Service test for City or Government jobs. The first one was for the Post Office, the second was in Kings County Hospital (in the 'G' Ward—which was for the insane), and the third was in a building across the street from the hospital where the doctors lived, who worked at Kings County. Well, thinking back on all that, I really had good choices. That's easy to say now 50+ years later. I turned down the scholarship and the 3 jobs as I knew that Steve wouldn't want me to work there and was expecting to marry me, so that meant no more school.

I guess after Tom went into the Navy I turned my attention to Steve. It's hard for me to say this, but the truth is that there was very little I liked about him, except for the fact that he was a hard worker. He actually worked 50 feet from his house. He worked in a small shop that did reupholstering. He had two sisters, one was older than him and the other was his twin. There were a total of eight children in his family. Steve's bedroom was a closet, literally, as his twin bed took up the whole room. No one in his family liked me except for the youngest whose name was Peggy. Peggy was about seven years old and maybe in second grade. She was always very quiet and really looked forward to my visits. I used to go over there after school and read to Peggy and help her with her homework. I remember one of the last days I saw Peggy, she was sitting in the dining room and right away I knew something was wrong. Her face looked like something had drained the life out of her. I tried to talk to her but she would not give me eye contact or even acknowledge that I was there. I asked Steve's mother what was wrong with her and she said "nothing". I went there for about a week afterward and each day she looked worse than she did the day before. She had stopped eating. But the look on her face was the thing that got to me. And why didn't anyone else see the change in her. It was so apparent that something happened to her but she was just ignored. At least that's the way I saw it. During the next few years, Peggy declined as they put her in a diaper and spoon-fed her. Eventually they put her in a nursing home where she lives to this day. It was a shame that they didn't even ask her what happened 'that day', the day they saw a change in her, or maybe they did and since it wasn't my business they kept it to themselves.

Steve's father was a Greek immigrant and hardly ever spoke a word. I remember that he used to come home very late every night and had his own room. The mother was also an immigrant from Greece who lived in a convent there with the nuns. I never heard why. The father never said one word to me and really I don't remember if the mother ever said anything to me either. His father was quite a bit older than his wife (maybe 20 years). He appeared to be 70 years old and she an 'old' 50. I think the only time I ever saw her in shoes was at my wedding (I think). Steve's twin sister never spoke to me either. Even when we were married she would call the house and say, "Put my brother, Steve, on the phone," never saying hello to me. In the beginning I would answer her by saying, "Okay, I'll get him," but after a while, I just put the phone down and went and got him. That went on for 13 years which was the length of time I was with him. And the funny thing is, when I just put the phone down instead of answering her, I felt like I was being rude. I was always an outsider in that family. When Steve and I bought a house in Long Island, he couldn't put my name on the mortgage since at the time I was only 20 years old and not 21 years old, which was the law then. But even after reaching 21 and throughout the marriage whenever I brought it up, Steve always had an excuse as to why he couldn't put my name on the deed. That house was his, not mine, and that's the way I felt throughout my entire marriage.

Going back to the New Year's Eve before the wedding in April, we had gone to a party that a friend of ours was giving. There was a girl in my school that I had chosen to be my maid of honor and invited her and her sister to this party. Well, I have always been a modest person and dressed that way, but this girl (the maid of honor) had worn a low-cut dress and she was top-heavy, so a lot was showing. From the time she got to the party until midnight, Steve kept staring at her boobs. I mean not just a glance, but the way he would look at her made me feel sick. At midnight the person who was having the party turned all the lights off and being in the basement, it turned completely black. Steve let go of my hand and I had no idea where he was—but I felt sick. The lights went back on and he was next to her. I wanted to throw up. I went to leave but he followed me and I took off my engagement ring and threw it down. I told him it was over and told him why. He didn't deny it but he began to cry. I could never stand to see a man cry so I took the ring back. Well, that was just the beginning of the ride I took with him.

At that time I was 17 years old and still living with the parents. I was out of the house a lot, almost every night after work. By then I had a job at the Brooklyn savings bank in the mortgage department as a secretary to a loan officer. I had a desk right outside his glass walled office. He would always be staring at me when I was typing or going through papers to file. He had a chair right next to his desk where I would sit to take steno notes. He would rub my leg sometimes. Now here, I was in another situation. I honestly didn't know if that was the way it was supposed to be or if that was wrong. If I stopped him, would I get fired? Does everybody do that? Would I be in trouble if I said anything and who would believe me or even listen to me? I had no physical boundaries. What are people allowed to do to me? When it came to things like that, I was confused. I would feel one way but thought another.

When I moved to Long Island with Steve, I changed my job which paid better in order to help make the mortgage payment. Still in Manhattan, it was an advertising agency where I was secretary to the president of the company. Right after we moved, my brother called to ask if he could bring his then wife to stay with us for a while. Tom was still in the Navy when he got married to this girl and got her pregnant. She was two months pregnant at the time and a little bit of a girl. Tiny in stature and definitely did not look pregnant. Of course I couldn't turn my brother down. At that time every day Steve and I drove to Manhattan for work and so she hitched a ride with us to the city and met us after work for a ride home. I didn't know where she went but she talked about a modeling agency. Who knows? She was a very strange girl. When she sat on the toilet, she would leave the bathroom door open. One day we woke up and my husband said he was 'sick' and couldn't go to work. He had never taken a day off from work and, in fact, he used to boast about it. And that same day my brother's wife didn't want to travel to the city either. I felt sick but didn't want to believe that this was done on purpose. Well, that evening something had happened in New York City and with all the traffic, it took me five hours to get home. I was so rattled by the detours, the black traffic lights, and the loss of direction I'd been through, that I went to bed as soon as I got home. I knew in my gut that they had slept together. Why I stayed with him at that point, I don't know. But where would I have gone? I had no backup plan. My younger brother still lived with the parents, and I knew that I didn't want to go back there so I just put it all out of my mind which has always been easy for me to do. I'm not sure how long she stayed with us until Tom picked her up but it felt like years. 15 years later they found her dismembered body in a dumpster in Baltimore. My brother and she had been divorced for years but she did give birth to a girl, whether it was my brother's or my husband's, I don't know. And I also don't know whatever happened to the child. My brother and I had a very strained relationship after he left the Navy.

I have to say that one of the few best times in my life was when I gave birth to my children. When I had my first two girls, I was married to Steve. It was a perfect marriage. He worked and I stayed home with my babies. Steve and I had very little to do with each other. He came home and I served him dinner on the TV tray so he could watch his program, Star Trek. The children seemed like a bother to him so the children and I sat in the kitchen together and had dinner. I was 'allowed' to go wherever I wanted and to buy whatever we needed. The girls and I went out every day—the playground, Jolly Rogers (an amusement park), petting zoos, Bethpage Restoration, and wherever else we wanted to go. My husband owned a beautiful split-level story home with a laundry room and finished basement, and he put in a built-in swimming pool in the back. I believe that it started bothering me that my children did not have a father who participated in their lives. He was not a nice person when we would argue and once he threw me on the bed and attempted to strangle me. I remember that I couldn't breathe and got to the point of death versus life, the second I chose life, a surge of energy ran through my body and I threw him off me. I actually became so angry that I scared him, but it was kind of a crazy anger. I could actually feel a separation of my anger from my body as if I had no control—the anger took over. Another time this happened was when we had a fight and he hit me over the head with a frying pan. It sounds funny now but I picked up the phone—it was a wall phone in the kitchen—and was going to call 911 when he approached me with his pan again. I looked directly at him and said, "You take one more step near me and I will kill you." Well, he believed me, and even scarier was that I believed it myself. My older daughter was standing at the bottom of the stairs and witnessed this. She was probably 6 years old at the time.

A short time after this we had acquired a 16 Lane Bowling Alley where I had worked running the desk, tending bar, and even learned a little bit about the automatic pinsetters and could retrieve a stuck ball. Another time that Steve became physical with me was when we were leaving the bowling alley one day and began arguing. About what—I don't remember. Well, he took hold of my hair and dragged me on the ground across the parking lot to the car. I screamed but no one came to help me and I knew that they wouldn't, as we were their 'bosses'.

Thinking back, the thing that disgusted me the most about him, aside from his extramarital whatever, was that whenever he wanted to have sex, he wouldn't say anything or do anything to lead up to that, as in foreplay, he would just get out of bed and lock the bedroom door. I cringed every time I heard the sound of the lock. There was absolutely no romance and, of course, I never experienced an orgasm, just the pounding of his flesh against mine. I thought this was normal—and it was to me. It was around this time that I began thinking of Rich and daydreaming about how it would've been to be with him. I even looked him up and saw that he moved to Queens. I got up enough nerve to call the number one day and his mother answered. I calmly asked if Rich was home and she asked who I was. After I told her, she said, "Oh please, don't call here. He is so happy now and is married with two children." Well, first of all, I had no idea she even knew about me, and the way she sounded (almost frantic), made me realize that Rich must've been really hurt by me. That was a revelation. The fact that 'I' could hurt someone so much that even their mother was concerned about me talking to him. I would never in a million years think that anyone could care enough about me to feel pain. I cried and cried about Rich. I cried about the position I put myself in. I cried about how lonely I was. I cried about how unhappy I was. I felt a little different after that. I can't explain it but I just knew something changed in me. By that time, I had given birth to two adorable girls who had become my world—my only world.

About the bowling alley—it was about 50 miles away and I was in charge of the business end of things and he was the fix-it man. It was at this time, not to my knowledge, he met his girlfriend—who by the way is still with him to this day. This one I didn't find out about until years later. This part of my life is kind of fuzzy as there were a number of profound occurrences that happened in a very short period of time. I began working at the bowling alley in the evenings and my husband would get this 14-year-old babysitter to watch the girls when he went out. We also had a refrigeration company that Steve had started about a year before we purchased the bowling alley. We incorporated it and had three partners: Steve, his friend Bob, and me. We all took part in it. Steve and Bob went on service calls as it was an air-conditioning service, and I took care of the appointment setting and the books. Steve had met Bob at a job he had earlier in a bowling alley in the city. After ending his reupholstering career, Steve went to school in New Jersey to learn about automatic pinsetter mechanics for Brunswick machines. Bob was a BS type of guy who was also very lazy. He always tried to pull the wool over Steve's eyes but I always saw it happening.

Steve was the one who suggested that I work at the bowling alley to save money on labor and so that we would know what was going on all the time. So anyway, working at the bowling alley changed me again. I wasn't this 'stay-at-home mom' anymore. I was feeling so confused and angry and not in control of my feelings. I had nobody to talk to so I could sort all this out.

So, one day, I was home with the girls and planning my day in my mind. Steve was leaving to go to work and asked me what I was going to do that day. So I told him I was going to clean the pool, go grocery shopping and do the wash. He said—with great authority—"NO! First you put in the wash, go grocery shopping, put the wash in the dryer, clean the pool, and then finish the wash." That second in time—and I'm not even sure if it was while he was talking or after he finished—something clicked in me. I don't know how else to put it but it happened in a second. I felt gone, lost, empty, confused, but mostly angry. In a split second, I realized that I 'loathed' this man. So much so that I felt sick if I looked at him. I had to get away from him—NOW. I honestly couldn't think straight—the overwhelming hatred I had for him controlled my every thought and move. Immediately, I told him I was leaving. When he said, "What about the kids?" I yelled, "Of course I'm not leaving them here!" He didn't say anything after that.

Linda was six at the time and Christine was three. It was an extremely difficult time for everyone, as we lived in the same house until he found me a house to rent which was about two miles from him. I wasn't thinking about anything else except getting away. My skin was crawling and I couldn't sit still for five minutes. I couldn't stay in his room and in fact, I couldn't sleep. I believe it took a week, but honestly, it could've been a month for him to find that place for us. In the weeks before I moved, he would give me money for food or whatever and wanted the receipt and every cent change back. One day he called his mother and twin sister over to the house and as you know, neither one of them ever talked to me, so when they did come over, they all sat in the living room by themselves. I was in the kitchen and heard mostly whispering but really didn't care why they were there and what they were saying. The one thing I did hear loud and clear was the mother saying, "Is she taking the kids?" The husband must've said yes as the mother replied, "Let her go—who cares." Well, there was no love lost there but she didn't even care about the kids? That hurt some.

So, I don't remember moving but I do remember not being allowed to take anything except my clothing and the children's clothing and their beds. The rental house was partially furnished with a kitchen table and chairs, a sofa, and a bed. I would drop off Linda at school and pick her up every day. I was beside myself. I couldn't function—nothing made sense. I suppose I did normal things with the children—I don't even remember. One night the husband called and wanted to come over and 'talk'. The girls and I had lived there for about two months by then. I told him, "Okay, I'll leave the front door open, as I have to take a shower." While I was in the bathroom, I heard a loud noise—like something had fallen. I yelled out "Steve" twice and no one answered. With my state of mind, I panicked, dried off, and got out of the bathroom. I yelled "Steve" again—no answer. I picked up something from the bathroom—it could've been anything, but I remember gripping this thing so tight that my hand hurt, and slowly made my way around the house. No one was there. By the time Steve got there I was so scared that I agreed to move back in with him when he suggested it. I didn't realize it at the time that it was really Steve's attempt to scare me. After moving back in the beginning, I felt safe. Feeling safe was my biggest priority at that time. A few months later I found out that I was pregnant again. Honestly, I wasn't as excited this time and hate that I felt that way, but I did, and more than that, I felt trapped again.

My girls had very little reaction to both moves as they both had very little to do with their father anyway. When we first moved out, I do remember Linda trying to figure out where their beds should be placed and checking out the backyard. But other than that I can't think of anything different about their behavior. Of course, Christine was only three years old at the time and I don't think it phased her at all. They were both 'mommy's' girls and if they thought it was all right with me, it was okay with them. And the move back to their father's home was just as though they had never left.

Upon moving back to the husband's house, my feelings were kind of put on hold—repressed. But again, working at the bowling alley was bringing new feelings to light. I wasn't this perfect wife and mother, housekeeper, cook, and chauffeur anymore; I was taking on a different role. It was one I wasn't familiar with and ran on energy that was created out of confusion, hatred, loneliness, and mistrust. It was as if I had a lot of power with no direction. My life as a mom completely changed. I had gotten to the point where I found myself leaving for the bowling alley earlier and earlier. The home became a confusing and angry place that I couldn't be around. I always felt like I was on the edge—of what I don't know—and I became very protective of that 'edge'. Then something happened and one day I woke up and just wasn't there—everything stopped—I remember sitting in the kitchen watching the second hand move on the clock—I swear it took about ten seconds for it to move one second. I knew something was wrong but really didn't care. Everything around me was going in slow motion—even Steve's yelling was muzzled—for lack of a better term.

I remember that Steve took me to a doctor and he asked questions like, "Where are you now—who is the president—what time is it?" Well, I don't really remember if I got anything right or wrong but what I do remember is that someone asked me whether it would be all right if I went to the hospital. "No, I'm not going to any hospital," I said. I visited this doctor three times a week—he was a psychiatrist. I don't ever remember talking to him or him talking either. No one in my family including my two brothers ever knew what was happening—I didn't even know what was happening but I guess life went on as before—whatever that was. Well, I guess Steve decided I should go back to work at the bowling alley and I guessed it was better than sitting in the kitchen, staring at the clock. He had hired a bookkeeper who got sick and he told me to take over her job. This is when I found out that he had been paying the babysitter every week even when she didn't work. I asked him about it and he just said, "She probably needs the money." So one night when I was home, he said he was going to the bowling alley. It was 3 AM and he wasn't home yet so I sat on the front stoop and waited. All of a sudden, I heard his Jeep about a block away—it had a distinct sound. It stopped, and I heard a door slam. I looked down the block and there was the babysitter coming out of her backyard and into her front door. The sound of the Jeep had begun again and I saw it emerge from around the corner, where her house was. I didn't say a word to him but the next day I stood outside the house and waited for her to ride past on her bike, on the way to her school. I saw her coming, got out in the street, and told her to stop. She did. I told her that I didn't want her seeing Steve as long as I am still living in this house. Her answer was, "We're not doing anything," implying that they haven't had sex yet. Well, that didn't seem to stop whatever was going on between them. I couldn't really blame her—at her age. I never confronted him about it—to me, it was what it was. I just felt so tired.

So, one night as I was tending to the bar at the bowling alley, I got a call from my husband telling me to close the bowling alley and come home. I got that same terrible feeling of being in trouble again. It had been Christine's birthday and we had a little party for her that afternoon. I had called Christopher earlier in the day to ask him and his new wife Lorraine to come but there was no answer. I had told my brother years before that I would name my second boy after him and when my first child was a girl, I knew my first boy would be named after his father, and I probably wasn't going to have more than three children, so I named my second girl after him. My brother's full name was Christopher Joseph and so I gave my second daughter the name Christine.

Anyway, I got home and saw my husband's face—I felt sick. He told me to sit down but I told him to "just tell me".

"Christopher drowned," he said. My initial thought was *what—you're not saying he's dead? No, I can't hear this; just don't say another word.* I pleaded in my thoughts, he can't be telling me that my baby brother is dead. But he said it, "He's gone." I hated him for saying that—and remember dropping to the floor. My strength left me. I was empty, confused, and angry, all at once. We got the babysitter to come over and left to go to Brooklyn where the parents lived and met Tom at their apartment. Tom and the father wouldn't let me go to the morgue to identify him. I thought maybe there was a mistake—it could've been someone else—NO—not Christopher, my baby brother. My mind was flooded with emotions and thoughts: *Why didn't I go to that party he had invited me to or to the off-Broadway show—why hadn't I called him the day before Christine's birthday?* I remember looking out the window of the parents' apartment when they went to identify him and feeling angry just seeing the world going on as if nothing happened.

I remember dressing for the wake—the first time I would see him dead, and picking out an outfit that would look good on me—for him. This was all like a dream—a real nightmare—but deep down inside I had this sick feeling of reality—and every time that reality hit me I would push it away—this couldn't be real. I wasn't there for him—to protect him—how could this happen—it was all so surreal. To this day, 43 years later, I can still feel that pain—the denial— the anger—the loss. After that my life became split. When I said anything, it was either before (his death) or after. When I spoke to the psychiatrist, I spoke in those terms. This became a life changer for me. I must've been in bed after that for months—I couldn't deal with anything—not my children, definitely not the husband or anything else that should have mattered. Again, 'they' wanted me in a hospital. Then one night while I was in bed, I woke up and was standing on the beach. At that moment I knew that my body was in bed but it all seemed okay. I could see the waves and out of the corner of my right eye, I spotted something shiny, and as I turned my head, I saw a black shiny limousine. As the back door opened, immediately I was there, and bending down I saw Christopher. Just as I saw him, I found myself sitting next to him and looking him straight in his eyes. As I thought, *How does it feel?* I could hear those thoughts as I didn't speak them from my mouth, and so could Christopher. He looked so peaceful and happy as he said there is "no pain" and "no worrying". I immediately knew he was all right. As he turned to look out the back window, I also turned to see his wife walking up the beach toward us. Then he was gone. When I woke up, I felt different. This wasn't a dream—there was a completely different feel to this. My baby brother was okay and he let me know.

I began my life, but this time I was different. Even though my brother's passing took all the life out of me, it also gave me a new one. Somehow I became braver and stronger. It took a while to pull out of the hole I felt I was in when Christopher died, but now I felt like nothing in this world was able to hurt me worse than what I just went through. My marriage was over—I hated Steve.

After the first time I left Steve and then moved back with the girls, I had gotten pregnant with my son Steve Jr. With everything that was going on in my life—and I hate to say this—I really didn't want to be pregnant. I believe my husband got me pregnant on purpose, thinking that this would save our marriage. I don't think I ever really bonded with Steve Jr. which I regret to this day. He was such a cute little baby—blonde hair, blue eyes. The life was out of me at that point and I had nothing to give and the guilt of it all overwhelmed me. God gave me this beautiful child and I just couldn't give him what he needed.

I think it was about 4 months after Christopher died that I took my three children and got out. The kids were nine, six and two. It's funny, even though I had this new inner strength, I was still so unstable. I wasn't able to sit still for ten minutes. I began to go out at night to look for a job. I knew I had to get a job since Steve wasn't going to support me and when I left him I had no money at all. I had a job offer at a bank but they wanted me to go away for three weeks for training which I couldn't do. Steve wouldn't give me a dime. Oh, and by the way, the 15-year-old babysitter moved in the day I moved out. She came from one of those strange households where you never knew what was going on behind closed doors. I never saw her mother or her father—ever.

So, where do you go to look for a job at night, since I had to be home during the day for my children? The bars were the only place I could think of since I had bartending experience already. I met a girl who volunteered to babysit sometimes from my new neighborhood. I was a wreck—no money—no

41

job, and to top it off—I wasn't emotionally prepared to handle a family by myself. He did nothing to help me and didn't want the kids at his house. He began to drink and so did I. I guess it was a learned behavior for me. Anyway, we stayed at that first apartment for about two months—I had no way to pay the bills. I had to sell my wedding and engagement rings for food money. My mind was gone and I couldn't get a hold of my thoughts or feelings. Everything became a burden to me— all the kids were acting out and fighting. The littlest thing became unbearable—where do I go? What do I do? I had no friends, no family to help. Yeah, I probably felt sorry for myself at that time and I don't think that a day went by that I didn't cry. At this point if Steve had even acted nice or offered some kind of support, I would've gone back to that house. But he never even offered to take the kids out for a day. My life was over—I had no life at all at that point. I felt like I was so scattered that I needed to be sewn together but didn't even think that would help. I felt totally alone. Everyone expected something from me but I had nothing to give. I felt ashamed that I couldn't even be a mother to my children. I was a failure. Steve even stopped paying for my visits to the psychiatrist as he said, "I was only paying for you to get back to me, the way you were." Who was I? That wife who never complained— never argued—did what she was told and remained there for an angry man to beat or have sex with. I realize now that I was nothing but a slave—the one that took care of his things. I remember when I read that book about a man who had cancer. I read all his thoughts and how that gave him such a sense of freedom as no one was able to control that part of him (his thoughts). It was then that I realized that I could think anything at all and wouldn't get into trouble since nobody could hear my thoughts. This gave me a great sense of freedom. It's almost funny that I didn't discover that until I was 29 years old. I wondered why I hadn't known that before. Did I think people could read my mind or was I so afraid that it even stifled my own thoughts?

Everything changed for all of us. I know the kids were angry and at times became uncontrollable. I really just didn't know what to do at that point. I felt confused and anxious all the time—I really just wanted to die at that point—there was no light at the end of this tunnel—I couldn't stand myself. I began going to bars at night and in the back of my mind I would think and hope that maybe I would meet someone who would love me and take care of us. Of course, I never did. But I did meet this guy who told me about a bartending job opening in the next town over. I went there the next day. The bar was called 'The Brigadoon'. When I walked in, I asked the first person I saw where the boss was and he pointed him out to me. He was sitting at the end of the bar, appeared to be 45 years old, bald, heavyset, and had dark circles around his eyes. He looked very angry. His name was Rick. He had a glass of dark liquor without ice sitting in front of him as he took a drag on his cigarette, and as I walked toward him, he said, in this 'matter-of-fact' deep, raspy, and loud voice, "Can I help you?" I'm sure he couldn't tell how nervous I was, as I knew that this may be my only lifeline, so I pulled enough energy together to answer. "Hi, I'm Pat, and I heard you were looking for a bartender." He never even asked if I ever tended a bar before and said, "Can you start tomorrow?" I wanted to shout and cry and run home to tell my kids but just came out with a "Sure, what time?".

Thus began my career as a bartender. I began working the day shift, and to be honest I truly do not remember what arrangement I made for the kids. I was losing my role of a mother and felt like I was being thrown into a whirlwind of events and just being in this robotic state of confusion—kind of acting on impulses instead of having thought out actions which would include consequences. I felt like I had gained new strength and at that point, my priorities had changed. I remember during the first few weeks leaning over the bar while I was working and asking the customers how to make their drinks. I had to do this very nonchalantly, as the boss never left the bar and sat in the same seat all during my shift, in fact every shift. He never changed his angry look—I could never tell what he was thinking—if he liked me—if I was doing okay for him or what? Everything at home was unorganized and I felt separated from my children. I felt like a child myself but knew I wasn't. I felt exposed—I had no clarity—there were no rules or guidelines as to what was going on.

So growing up with the parents there were no rules either. They just made the rules up as they went along and that rule was only for that time and situation—so there were never any set rules. It always depended on their state at the time. It was nothing you could get used to as it changed all the time. But the one thing I did get used to was my constant state of fear. I guess the fear of the unknown. But, at least I did have a role in the parents' home when I lived there—the useless ugly daughter—the protector of the kids—the invisible student— King of the snow hill (nobody got up my mountain) apparently from repressed anger. There was no privacy in our home; we couldn't keep the door closed, even in the bathroom. It's probably why I have been constipated my whole life. They just walked in, no matter if anyone else was in the house or not. But I did have a role there—and in the marriage the role of a wife and mother, I knew what I had to do. The thought of where I would live or how I was going to eat never entered my mind. This was a whole different ballgame and I didn't know how to play.

So, one night Steve called me and wanted to meet with me to take care of some 'business'. We met at a restaurant and he pulled out some pieces of paper and told me to sign them and if I did he would start paying me $400 a month for child support. If I didn't sign—no money. So I signed over my portion of the bowling alley and refrigeration business. Also in the deal was our own home that he would get for us. So I thought—*a place to start—I wouldn't have to worry about that anymore.* Yeah, it did turn out to be a nice house but came with a nice sized mortgage. That $400 barely bought us food, much less the mortgage payment, electric, water, phone, gas, etc. What good was a beautiful nice house with no furniture and no way to pay the expenses that came with it.

By this time, I had met a guy named Dean. He was a construction worker, Italian guy with the slicked back hair.

He would come into the bar and have a couple of drinks; he would talk a little with other customers and never overstayed or got drunk. He was very handsome to me and would call me Missy. He seemed okay and was never flirty but came off as a kind of serious person. He stood about 6'2" and about 200 pounds. Mind you, my mind was never wanting to find a boyfriend for me, but a husband and father to my children. So he seemed nice in the beginning—even came over to my house and made 'Italian gravy' as he called it. It was spaghetti sauce—but it was good. So one night we were out having a few drinks and out of nowhere he made this 'arggg' sound very loudly. He was playing shuffleboard and as I turned to look at him he took the heavy metal puck and threw it at me and if I hadn't have ducked, it would've hit me in the head. He had this ugly angry look on his face and yelled for me to "Get over here". Fear came over me and I froze. When he started to come around the bar toward me, I ran and shouted to the bartender and the customers with a pleading voice, "Someone call 911, please." No one moved—not even the manager of the bar. I was scared. *This guy is crazy*, I thought. We didn't have an argument or anything that may have caused him to act like this—at least in my mind. He was terrorizing me at this point as he grabbed my arm, swung me around, and punched me in my face so hard that he knocked one of my teeth out. He hadn't knocked me down, so I flew out of the bar door hoping someone outside would help me. I was running toward Hempstead Turnpike when he caught me by my hair and pulled me in his car. I thought real quick *maybe it's over now,* but while I was still hoping for an end to this mad man's rampage, he backhanded me maybe two or three times in the face and head. I remember falling forward and landing on the floor of the car. I lay there—not moving—with the thought that maybe he'll think I'm dead and leave me alone. I lay still for maybe 10 minutes while he was still driving. He never pulled over to see if I was okay or even call my name. I'm not going to lie—I did feel stunned but I'm not sure if that came from the physical beating I just took or the idea of the horror that just happened. That whole thing just took me by surprise and was beginning to feel surreal. I finally began slowly to sit back up half expecting to get hit again when I saw that he was driving me home. When he pulled his car in my driveway—neither of us said anything—I got out and went into my house. Thank goodness the kids were asleep. I closed and locked the door behind me and stood there until I heard him pull the car out and leave. I went to the bathroom and washed the blood off my face and for the first time looked at my face with a front tooth gone and cried for the first time that night. "How could I have let this happen?" I wasn't sure of anything at that point—should I quit my job?—Are we even safe? What was I thinking? I know I couldn't predict something like this but that night the world became an even scarier place.

Yeah, so I quit my job and got another bartender job about two miles away. It was a little bit classier. Dean kept calling but I never answered. He came over to the house a few times—my car was outside so he knew I was home but we just sat in the house and kept quiet until he left. One day after work as I was sitting at the end of the bar counting my tips, in walked Dean. I didn't want to go to the trouble of explaining who he was so I left the bar to get in my car, but he was right behind me and took my arm to turn me around. "Get your hands off me," but before I knew it a guy came from behind Dean and pushed him away as he yelled "Get off of her". Dean was not about to get pushed so he took a swing at this guy. The guy was about my age, tall, lanky, and fast as he ducked and landed a punch that knocked Dean toward to the ground. He then kicked him and said, "Don't ever come near her again." I knew he meant it and so did Dean, I think. I took off after I quickly gave my thanks to this guy. I had never seen him before that day but I was more worried about Dean beating me back to my house so I took off and went home. I didn't hear from him or see Dean that night so I went to work the next day. I was very anxious but calmed down after a few hours when I didn't see Dean. Then all of a sudden, in walked the guy who saved me the night before. He introduced himself as "I'm George. Are you all right?" Well, I thanked him properly this time and asked him how he knew about Dean. He said, "Word gets around fast in these neighborhoods. I heard about you quitting the Brigadoon and getting this job because of this guy. I just happened to be coming to see who they were talking about when I saw you outside. I said to myself, 'This stops now.'" What a nice guy. He gave me his telephone number and said, "If he ever bothers you again, just call me."

Dean did call me that night and told me he was coming over—I told him not to but he sounded urgent. I immediately called George and he was there within 20 minutes. He parked behind my car in the driveway. Dean had come by about 11 PM and so I told George he could go home but he insisted to "stay just in case". Honestly, I felt better with him there. He left early in the morning and I was off that day but about 5 o'clock there was a knock at the door. I looked out the window and there was Dean with his left leg in a cast and holding crutches. His face was black and blue and he pleaded for me to open the door—I did. I felt sorry for him. Well, we ended up talking and he said he had an idea. He said we could open up our own bar so I wouldn't have to worry about where I worked. It seemed like a good idea at the time. The first thing he did, though, was to have me call George and tell him that I decided to give Dean another chance—which I did. Dean put up the cash and I got the liquor license—as he said he was not allowed to get one—and he never told me why. He named the bar 'BBs pub'. Everything seemed to be going all right for quite a few months until one day he suddenly changed—again. I kind of saw it coming as he began to clean the bar and put the ashtrays down harder than usual. This inner body chill began in my stomach—I knew something was not right. Very slowly I began to walk to the door as there was no one in the bar at the time. He ran from around the bar and grabbed me just before I got to the end of the bar within feet from the escape door. He threw me down to the floor and put a knife to my throat and shouted, "You were going to leave me, right?"

"No," I shouted back, "I wouldn't do that." He pressed on the knife and I felt the blade against my skin but I had learned patience from my childhood so I lay there quietly. All I could think of was my children. *What would they do without me— who would take care of them?* I went through in my mind how each one of them would react when they heard that I was dead. When you're under pressure, you wouldn't believe how fast your mind could go. I thought of each one of the children and how their lives would change—all of these thoughts flooded my mind and, actually, these thoughts became more important than this sharp object that threatened my life. It's funny how things work. I'm guessing that if Dean had slashed my throat at that point, I would've felt nothing. Just as fast as Dean had transposed, he returned, got up, and said, "Get out of here." He didn't have to tell me twice. I walked quickly out the door, got in my car, and drove down the block to the first bar I saw. I was a wreck.

I ordered a vodka and 7-Up and drank it down in one gulp. There was this guy in there who said, "Take it easy—it can't be that bad." His name was Gary. Well, I began to tell him my story when who walks in but Dean. He demanded, "Go outside with me." When I said "no", he came at me to grab me and this guy that I was just talking to tried to put his arm around Dean's neck to overtake him but Dean knocked him on his butt. That was enough, though, for Dean to storm out of the bar. I had a couple of more drinks before I went outside to discover four of my tires were flat. Dean had used that knife to slash them. The guy I had been talking to followed me out and saw this. He told me to go back inside and that he would be right back. I have no idea where this guy was going. Was he going after Dean—who was this guy? Well, about an hour later he walked in and introduced himself as Gary and said, "It's okay to go out now." Still bewildered, I went outside and there was my car with four 'new' tires. He just said you can go now. Wow! What do you say to a person like this? He went and got me four tires and changed each one of them—for me. I asked him if I could buy him a drink for what he had done and he answered, "Sure." Well, we must've talked for hours as I told him everything—well, everything about Dean and me. He tells me that he owns a house in Islip that has three

48

bedrooms and offers to move us into the house. He said, "I'm hardly ever home anyway and you won't even have to work since I am paying all the bills anyway. You could use the $400 for food for you guys." It was really gutsy of me but I knew I couldn't go on with Dean's threats and how it must be affecting the kids. "Yes," I said, "when can you do this?"

"Tomorrow," he said— so I went home and told the kids we're moving. Of course my kids had no idea how Dean had been treating me. They were all excited as was I. Mind you, I wasn't attracted to this guy but my gut knew he was someone I could trust—like George. So, he shows up with this moving truck and two guys and within an hour and a half I was following him in my car to his house. *This was pretty far,* I thought, as I never drove this far in Long Island. And the house and area were definitely a big downgrade from where we were living but the advantages outweighed the disadvantages immensely. So, Islip became our new home and Gary became my new boyfriend. I felt so grateful to this man. It seemed like the kids adapted very well as I got them registered into the Islip school district. But, even with this arrangement, I wasn't happy. By this time I had developed 'clinical depression' which I may have had for a long time but never really noticed.

I would get up to get the girls ready for school but had to go back to bed until noon when my son caught the bus for kindergarten. I felt so guilty—I would put the TV on for him and instead of spending time with him, I would sleep. I knew he wasn't happy but this feeling of doom overtook me. I didn't know what to do or even if there was anything I could do. Today they had medications for everything, but back then you wouldn't talk about things like that, at least I didn't. Deep down inside I just didn't feel right, but I guess I should say I had never felt right.

As a kid, I was always on my guard and never relaxed. I always had that 'knot' in the pit of my stomach. I knew I was different even then and watched how other kids had friends, told secrets, and appeared relaxed around other kids and their parents. I was never like that and knew I couldn't be—I believe they all had basic instincts which I didn't possess. I was always the outsider and those feelings never left me. I never 'outgrew' them. So, I believe all this and everything else I experienced turned into this dark gloom of depression which I didn't know how to deal with.

And then it happened—I found out I was pregnant. By this time, Gary never came home after he finished his job and by the time he got home about midnight, he was drunk and just fell into bed. The only time I saw him was on Saturdays and Sundays; we did do things every weekend—he didn't like staying at home—we would go fishing, take a ride upstate, or go to concerts. But these things never involved my own children. His belief was that 'kids can raise themselves'. And he always sounded convincing. He had a child from his first marriage and I think he saw him every two or three months. At least that's when he brought him over to the house. His son got along fine with my kids. So when Gary found out I was pregnant he accepted that fact—what else could he do? There was no way I would have ever considered an abortion. At that time I had been playing in a 26+-year-old adult soccer league as a goalie. I had gotten involved through someone that I had met at one of my children's soccer games. I had been playing for maybe three seasons when I discovered my pregnancy and quit. I was happy to know that I was going to be a 'mommy' again but for some reason did not picture Gary as a 'daddy'. For one thing, he was never home—and another—he never liked being home. I felt a little scared.

My kids were so excited to have a baby brother or sister, especially the girls who were now 13 and 10 years old. The pregnancy went along well up until about my sixth month when I noticed that I wasn't as big as I expected to be; after all, I had three children already and knew what I should look like by my sixth month. My doctor said everything looked fine but by my seventh month I knew there was something wrong—I just wasn't gaining weight. By this time, I had thought it out and did not want my child being born without a legal father, I told Gary I wanted to be married to him— romantic, huh? I really don't think he wanted to but we did get married. I feel that if I hadn't gotten pregnant we would not have gotten married. So, he did the right thing when I was in my seventh month. We had a very small gathering at the house that was just family. I wasn't ecstatic but felt at ease knowing that this child would have a legal father. All this happened within the first three years of when we first met. All the while, the gnawing feeling of guilt had never left me from childhood. No matter what I did—I always felt like I was in trouble—and here I am again in a pregnancy that doesn't feel right and a marriage that really, neither of us wanted. Gary never treated me any differently because I was pregnant but my children were very excited about having a new brother or sister.

I remember this one time I was in the grocery store and this young, maybe 12 or 13-year-old girl, that had Down's syndrome, came running down the aisle toward me after letting go of her mother's hand and giving me this really big hug. I thought that was so sweet but it was soon after that that my oldest child asked me very seriously what I "would do if there was something wrong with the baby". Now my daughter wasn't with me when this child had come up to me and hugged me. My answer to her was, "This is our child—our family's child, and it wouldn't make a difference to me." It seemed kind of odd that both of these incidents happened around the same time but they both seem so natural. So, I began to have labor pains in my eighth month and was very aware that this pregnancy was not like any other and that there was something wrong. So my neighbor Judy drove me to the hospital (Stony Brook). There were no cell phones at the time, so there was no way to know which bar Gary was in to let him know that I was about to have the baby. I'm guessing that Judy told him when he got home. So, when I was in the hospital, I remember arriving there and being in pain and the next thing I remember is asking this doctor why he was making a line on my stomach with what felt like a sharp pencil and then hearing "put her out". Then nothing until waking up to find out that my baby had been in 'fetal distress' and that they had to take her out by way of a C-section. Gary was there when I woke up and looked sad, so I asked him, "Did my baby die?"

"No," came a calm voice from the other side of my bed, "you have a daughter and she weighs 4 pounds and 12 ounces."

Not a bad weight, I thought to myself, *for a premature baby.*

He, being the doctor who delivered the baby, went on to say—which did concern me—"At first I thought she was one of those 'floppy' children." My heart dropped—but he explained that when I lifted up her arm and it didn't just flop down, I realized that I was wrong. "But we do have to do some testing on her."

"What kind of testing?" I asked.

He said, "Genetic testing, because there is definitely something not right with her."

"Is she brain damaged?" I asked.

"Yes, but we really don't know the extent of it yet."

I was devastated. I spent hours and hours crying and trying to think and remember what it was that I had done during the past eight months that may have caused this. I thought I was so careful going on this health food binge and vitamin diet. I had stopped smoking, drinking, and smoking weed which Gary had introduced me to a couple of years earlier. I wanted this baby to be so healthy and didn't want to take any chances.

I couldn't bring myself to face my child since I was feeling so much guilt. Every time a nurse would come in to this room to ask me if I wanted see her, I would just cry. Nobody could fix this—I hurt one of my own children—I didn't know how. I think it was by the end of her second day of life that my heart opened up to my lonely child. By this time she weighed 4 pounds and 6 ounces. They handed me th' 'ttle creature and the tears just rolled down my face. 'he most beautiful baby I ever laid eyes on—so soft. I told her how sorry I was if it was my fault. e felt safe in my arms. After I was released from 'e wasn't ready to come home yet and so I went back every day to hold my baby and talk to her. Her body weight went down to 4 lb 2 oz so she spent the next 40 days of her life in an incubator. She finally came home at 4 lb 15 oz. Patty Ann was a special child that had to be fed every two hours for the first 4 to 5 months. We had to get a special nipple for her as she was so tiny. Instantly my priorities changed and she came first in my life. Patty Ann got 24-hour care from me. Her cry was very faint, as she was weak. Her first smile came at about nine months old and WHAT a smile! Her whole face lit up and her body kind of pulled together—there was a whole body smile. When Gary was home, he would try to put together things that would capture her attention and hang them from the ceiling like a mobile to enable her to develop her cognitive abilities.

The genetic testing came back only to find that Patty Ann had been created with her number 10 chromosome defective which was genetic and had been passed down—and it really doesn't matter where it came from—but now I know that it wasn't something I did wrong and at that point none of that really mattered. Patty Ann was Patty Ann and we all loved her. She became a big part of our life and we took her everywhere. By the time she was nine months old, she was enrolled in a school where she received physical therapy, speech therapy, occupational therapy, and around other children who had similar disabilities. Truthfully, though, I don't believe she understood enough to relate to them. Her family was her whole world. One night when Patty Ann was propped up in her infant seat, around 1 ½ years old, Gary's mother had called and I was on the phone with her, as Gary had come home drunk and was passed out in the bed, and talked with her for a few minutes. While still on the phone I walked back to the living room with the phone in my hand and saw Patty Ann slumped over. Her face was blue—I picked up her limp body, threw down the phone, and screamed for Gary. He didn't wake up so I went back to the phone, picked it up, and his mother was still on the phone. I screamed at her to get off the phone and she wouldn't listen but kept asking, "Is Gary all right, is Gary all right?"

I yelled, "Your Gary is passed out and I need to call for an ambulance for Patty Ann so get the fuck off the phone!"

After what seemed an eternity, she finally got off the phone and I called 911. I put Patty Ann on the table and knew her life was in my hands. I picked up her frail body, lifted up her neck and blew a puff of air into her mouth. I did this a couple of times and finally felt a warm breath from her body come out. Just at that time, the EMTs came in and took her from me into the ambulance. I followed the ambulance to the hospital. My Patty Ann had lived. I couldn't stop crying as they placed my baby back into my arms.

At 2 ½ years old, Patty Ann weighed only ten pounds. She knew who I was as she would cry if I would walk past her chair. Her eyes could never focus, as they rolled left and right and she still had poor coordination but could hold onto her bottle in order to feed herself. At about the age of a year and a half, Patty Ann had an operation on her eyelids as she was so weak that she couldn't keep her eyes open. After the operation she was able to keep her eyes open and we thought that she would be more stimulated now—which in fact she probably was.

Then one day, Patty Ann had a runny nose. Gary told me to keep Patty Ann home that day but I was the one caring for her day and night—not him—so decided to send her to school anyway. She came home that afternoon with her tiny nose so stuffed that it was hard for her to breathe. We had bought a nose syringe for her in times like this—she hated it when I would use the syringe but it was something that had to be done once in a while. She became worse overnight and the next day she was in the hospital.

As I was writing about Patty Ann's Peanut life for this book, my emotions became so strong that I completely forgot to mention two of the most important happenings in my life. When Patty Ann was about five months old, I discovered I was pregnant again. I was ecstatic knowing that Patty Ann would be having a brother or sister of her own age. The youngest of my children, from Steve, was ten years old already so I felt blessed to be pregnant again. But this time I knew that there was a possibility that a genetic misalignment could happen. There was a social worker from the hospital when Patty Ann was born who had kept in touch with me and so I went in for an amniocentesis in my fourth month. The genetic testing itself takes two months. The waiting was grueling for me. So in my sixth month I got a call from a social worker, who told me on the phone that this child was going to be all right. So when we went to meet with her, she explained that this child was a carrier, as his number 10 chromosome was upside down but aligned—but that if he were to have a child, there was a one in four chance that the child would be completely healthy, be a carrier, be like Patty Ann, or be profoundly brain-damaged, as records showed that another child born with that same brain damage lived to be only 18 days old. The social worker explained the difference and even showed actual photographs of the male and female chromosome number 10 and how they could possibly meet at conception. So, just knowing that this child would not have any brain damage gave me a great sigh of relief. And so, my second son, Joseph Christopher, was named after my brother as I had promised him. He was the biggest one of all at 9 lb 15 oz and 24 inches long. I had him through a C-section, as at that time the doctors believed that if you already had one C-section, every child after that had to also be a C-section. This was the best pregnancy ever—an appointment to give birth— no labor pains at all. I was so excited to have this child that I called him my 'miracle child'. His father was happy, too, but had changed—just as I had but still I only saw him on the weekends. And now I had five children. Two teenagers who had never gotten along and were always fighting—my 10-year-old son who by this time began acting out, as I couldn't give him the love and attention he needed so much—and my two babies—one of which needed 24 hour care. Even though I love my children more than myself, this deep-seated dark feeling of doom would not leave. I became more and more depressed and tired. Then the unthinkable happened. I found myself pregnant again. The only time I had used birth control was when I first got married at 18, and again after having Linda. I never used it again as there was so much controversy over its effects. I felt so guilt-ridden already—how could I have done this? Where did that strong girl go? All I felt was doom—it enveloped me. I knew I was a horrible mother and person. There was no way out for me—I was in this dark endless tunnel. This was the beginning of my serious thoughts of suicide. It wasn't that I felt sorry for myself—I loathed myself. All the negative words that were said to and about me were true—I was a bad person; who was I trying to kid all these years. I was given everything but couldn't handle it. I believe even God turned his head from me. I could truly solve everyone's problems if I just wasn't here anymore.

And one night I faced all these thoughts. I went out for a drive and found myself on the parkway at night in the pouring rain, probably driving at 80 mph, and all of a sudden, I saw a cement bridge. I could actually picture my car crashed up against the cement structure and as fast as I was driving, my mind was running 1000 times faster. I could see Linda's face when she was told about me, at the same time, her life with her father flashed in front of me. She would be happier in the long-run. This happened with each one of my children one by one and in the end they would all be happier. This probably all flashed through my mind in a split second. But, wait, Patty Ann came back to my mind, and instinctively I knew that no one would be able to love her and give her all the care that I could and—WOOSH—I passed the bridge. It wasn't that I loved Patty Ann more than any of my other children, but it was that she was the one who needed me and wouldn't do as well without me. Whether that was true or not I don't know, but at that split second, it was true.

I pulled over to the side of the road and cried like I never cried before. I cried for what I almost did—cried for my children—cried for my brother Christopher—I cried for the past—I cried until I couldn't cry anymore. Then went home like nothing happened.

So I began the whole process again: the doctors, the social worker, the amniocentesis, the dreadful waiting period. I really didn't have a good feeling about this pregnancy. I mean, one in four chances, of a healthy baby. I was tired—just really tired. And then it came—the dreaded phone call from the social worker.

"Just tell me that she's okay," as I did know I was having a girl.

"You should come into the office," she answered.

That's all I remember until my neighbor found me wandering in the middle of the street. Judy, who had lived across the street and kind of befriended me, saw me looking dazed and ran over asking me loudly, "Are you alright—are you okay?"

When I heard her, it felt like I just woke up, but not all the way up. I felt like I was in a faraway dream. The next thing I knew, I was sitting in her car as she was asking me to pick one of my children to go with me to the hospital. I chose Christine as she was the logical one which is what went through my mind. Somewhere deep inside me I knew I was in trouble and could count on Christine. For what?—I don't know. Linda was home and took care of the other children. Gary wasn't home. I remember not speaking all the way to the hospital. My thoughts were scattered and fleeting. I couldn't hold on to one thought. Next thing I remember was feeling awake and staring at the social worker. She was talking in a very deep tone that dragged on. It was as if I were watching a slow-motion picture. And from nowhere a doctor appeared asking me these silly questions. I know I knew the answers but couldn't quite grasp them.

"Would you like to stay here in the hospital for a while?" came out loud and clear.

"No," I said, thinking of my kids at home. At the time I didn't quite understand what was going on but felt safe with Judy and Christine. On the trip home I guess I came back to reality a bit when I heard Judy say "I am so sorry—if there is anything I can do."

"No," I answered robotically, "I'll be okay—thank you." This is when I first realized that the baby that I was carrying—was not okay. When we got back, I went to bed and fell asleep. The next day the phone rang—it was a social worker. When she said, "We can't wait too long—you have to make up your mind," it came to me all at once. This baby will have the worst damage of all—the oldest child ever, who had this condition, lived to be 18 days old, with a ventilator and all kinds of tubes. I can't put my baby through that—I could feel my loss instantly—it became hard to breathe and my eyes welled up—my guilt overwhelmed me. She wants to know if I want to kill my baby. All kinds of things went through my mind—I was going through the five stages of grief in a flash when suddenly it came to me.

"When can you do this?" I asked somberly.

There was no thinking it over—I would never want a baby to go through that. I may have given up my soul at that point. That next week was kind of hazy until I found myself alone in a small cold room with this IV in my left arm. I knew that the injection that the doctor was going to push in the IV was 'literally' going to kill my baby. Before he came into the room, I took this time to talk to Annie, which I named her. I told her how sorry I was that she would never take a breath of air—never meet her sisters and brothers—never feel the warmth of a human body. I also told her of the reasons for my decision. Maybe that was just to relieve my guilt, I don't know. Then I cried. The doctor then came in and gave me that fatal dose of death. After that I went through natural childbirth as I felt the labor pains. But, these were different than what I had felt before. This time I knew I was giving birth to a dead child. She wouldn't cry after birth—I wouldn't be taking her home to her family, wouldn't be putting all those cute little outfits on her. I would be leaving her, here, in this hospital.

So, after it was over, they unexpectedly came into my room with this tiny infant swaddled in a blanket and placed her in my arms. Her skin had not even been developed yet but I could plainly see the resemblance of Annie and Patty Ann. I really didn't have much to say to her at that time, as I felt drained and had probably said all that I wanted to her already.

That was in January. It was the following May that Patty Ann got so sick that she had to be hospitalized. She had pneumonia. Patty Ann was in the hospital for 3 months in the ICU most of that time. I clearly remember that day when they told me that Patty Ann was ready to go home. She was wearing a cute little blue dress and was so happy as she smiled and moved her legs. I had never seen my baby as happy as I had seen her when she saw me walk into her room at the hospital. Patty Ann absolutely knew she was going home. I just stood at the door with the nurse, doctor and Social Worker in the room with Patty. This feeling of dread came over me and I instantly knew that I was taking her home to die. I even said it aloud, "I'm taking her home to die."

"No," they all said. "Look at her. She's all better." But I knew better deep in my soul. In fact I couldn't even hold her. The hospital sent a nurse home with us and she sat in the back seat holding my Patty Ann. The nurse fed Patty Ann and put her to bed that night. I didn't know why but I hadn't even touched her the entire night. It was about 11pm when I was on my way to bed that I placed my hand over her forehead and felt her body warmth. At 6am I woke up and she was gone. My Patty Ann—gone. There are no words to describe my feelings of emptiness, horror, fear, unbelief and total surrender of my soul at this time or ever. She was gone.

It was soon after this that Gary left. He just left—didn't even bother to come back to get his clothes. He was never home anyway, so his presence wasn't missed. So, jobless again my ex gave me a job at the bowling alley—and this is when I was first introduced to cocaine. By whom, I don't remember. The following four years were a conglomerate of events that one would expect in the life of a drug addict who was also very much aware of how she was destroying her family but so overcome with depression, fear, loneliness, anger, guilt, and by this time was caught in the undertow of this giant wave of self-loathing and saw no way out. So I just continued as if this was meant to be my new life. No one seemed to notice or even care or even reprimand me—I guess I just assumed that they knew what I was going through. A generalized 'they' which included my children and anyone else with whom I came into contact. I got to a point where I accepted that I was this wild, carefree, shell of a person. My worries and problems seem to delude me—I had forgotten that part of me who was a mother who put her children before herself—a mother who had suffered the loss of two children and two marriages—a child who had gone through sexual assault and abuse from the same people who should have loved and protected her. That person was gone. She was a pitiful, sad, lonely, non-assertive lost soul just going through the motions. That person would do anything not to confront the situation and would allow other people, even strangers, make simple decisions for her. At that time the people I came into contact with were probably just like me or maybe not but it didn't seem to matter— nothing seemed to matter. Every day ran into the next—I became anxious when I was home and wasn't able to take a deep breath. I was trapped into what had become a bundle of nerves. I knew what I wanted to do was stay home and be a mom again but just didn't know how. There was no one to turn to, as I was totally alone and out of control—and I felt it. My life didn't seem to matter. I knew in my heart that something big would happen—it was bound to.

Much of the next few years I can't really recall—just snapshots of a time and a place. I knew, though, that I just gave up at this point in my life—I was a different person— my bills weren't being paid. Somewhere in there I had signed divorce papers that would entitle Gary to $20,000 for the house, no part in his pension (which I didn't care about anyway), and the right to see his child whenever he wanted. I did want my child to know his father but it didn't matter as he only came around occasionally anyway. So I refinanced the house and gave Gary the $20,000 and was on my own again.

So, we spent five years there but soon got foreclosed. Before that happened, though, my mother had called me and had nowhere to live, so I picked her and her friend up and took them to my house. I had the garage in the home fixed up so that they can have their own place. By that time my oldest child Linda had been married and had two children. Linda was suffering, too, with two small children, already divorced, and having to work full-time. They came over quite a bit but I wasn't in any position to help her—I couldn't even help myself. I was still on drugs and going out every night and sometimes not coming home until the next day. My second child, Christine, had gotten a scholarship to Columbia College and had moved into their dorms. So one night about 3 AM I heard this knocking on my front door. It was Mac (my mother's friend) and he was looking very scared.

He said, "I think there's something wrong with your mother."

I quickly put some slippers on and went into the garage and there she was lying in bed shaking as if she were trying to reach her hand out to me. At that moment I knew there was something drastically wrong with her. "Mom, Mom, Mommy," I cried out as I took her hand. At that point I was a little girl and she was my mommy. I called 911 and had her in my arms and just as the EMTs rushed in, she stopped breathing. They began CPR on her, put her on a gurney and took her out into the ambulance. I followed in my car scared and crying as I got to the hospital, I was rushed into the waiting room. About 20 minutes or so went by when the doctor came in and told me, "We got her back a few times but weren't able to keep her. I'm sorry—she's gone."

"She's gone,"— that kept ringing in my brain. My father had died 11 years earlier but that didn't really faze me, but 'mom'—that helpless guilt-ridden mom. None of the bad things entered my mind at that time— 'Mommy was gone'.

I had to get away. I was so overwhelmed I couldn't breathe. For some odd reason I decided to move to Colorado. My third child Steve, who was 15 at the time didn't want to go with me. Linda begged me to let him stay with her and her two children and they would live in the house. Another big mistake I made. Linda was only 22-years-old at the time and her children were four and three years old. As much as Linda had good intentions, it was a bad decision on my part not to take Steve. But I could say that about my whole life up until now. So I rented a truck, filled it up, and took off with my youngest child Joey who was six at the time. We hit the road going to another state not knowing anyone and with no job waiting—what was I thinking? I just knew my head was exploding and I had to get away. Me and my baby—going to Colorado—who was I?

So, I'm not going to bore you with details of my two-year stay in Colorado, but what was amazing was that I began nursing school when I got back to New York. I got my LPN license which was unbelievable for me. It wasn't even a planned thing. I had gotten a job in a nursing agency as a human resource director. At that job someone who had the desk behind me had said, "Pat, why don't you become a nurse?" I guess I thought it was good idea at the time, so I did it—really was not my passion. Thinking back on it, I now say, "You never know what God has in store for you." I was still battling depression, drugs and alcohol. Still disappointing my children—still hating my life and unable to share my feelings with anyone. Even after passing the LPN boards I still felt lost. I guess I just resigned myself to feeling like a loser. Even my kids made fun of me. Of course it hurt me but I knew I deserved it. My thoughts and dreams of who I wanted to be had disappeared slowly over the years.

So again, something moved me. This time I was walking home after work in a snowstorm as my car had broken down. I got home and told my youngest child Joey to open up the map and find a place in Florida. "We're moving," I said. He looked at the map and pointed to Treasure Island which was on the West Coast of mid-Florida. Well, I happened to know of a patient I had a few years back telling me she was moving to St. Petersburg and if I was in the area to look her up. Well I did and she told me that Joey and I could stay with her until I got set up with an apartment. I put my belongings in storage and we flew there the next day. We only took a few changes of clothes with us. So we arrived there and were greeted by Mary who had been a patient of mine and got settled into her apartment. *This was great,* I thought. But, on the second day we were there, I went out for a walk with Joey to check out the city and when we got back the door was locked and she wouldn't answer the door. I went down to the apartment building management office and they told me, "I'm sorry but she doesn't want you there," WHAT??? Here it was about 5 PM in the evening, in a city I don't know, with a 14-year-old child and no money. The only thing that came to my mind, as I was beginning to panic, was to talk to the street people. We did and ended up at an old house run by the YWCA and a wonderful woman who welcomed us in and gave us our own room with bunk beds.

I'm guessing we lived there for about eight weeks in which time they helped me transfer my LPN license and child support to Florida. The first job I was presented with was at a Hilton hotel, working evenings as a bartender a couple of nights and the other nights doing room service. I didn't even look for a nursing job, as I felt I was comfortable there at the hotel and made decent money. The YWCA got us a one-bedroom apartment and we were on our feet again—but I was still plagued with the addictions. It didn't take me long to realize that this place was just as bad as anywhere else since I was the problem. I had no idea what was in store for us here. I went to work at the Hilton wearing a white shirt, bowtie, and black pants as that was their uniform. Even though I looked professional on the outside—inside I was still that 10-year-old girl afraid and feeling like I was in trouble all the time. I guess the alcohol made me act and feel more together than I really was. My poor Joey, left alone so often, this time without a brother or sisters. Those demons had a tight grip on me to the point of not even knowing how or caring to fight them.

Then something happened. The first apartment we lived in was on the second floor of a walk-up. I still had no car so we were walking around the area and as we were on our way home, a car pulled up next to us. It was a downstairs neighbor of ours and he asked if we needed a ride home. We got in the car and he asked us if we believed in God and Jesus and then asked if we believe that Jesus was God's Son on earth. Of course I believed that and I just assumed that Joey did also. We both responded with "Yes". Well, right there in this virtual stranger's car—Joey and I were saved. I felt a sense of peace come over me like nothing I ever felt before. Not only did this man bring us to the Lord but he also gave us Bible study lessons for about six months in his home. He even gave us our own Bibles. I listened to his every word and every letter and to this day I remember his teachings. His name is Bob. We lived at this apartment for about a year and a half until I met a woman at work who invited us to live at her house. But the thing was that the second we moved, Bible study was gone. It had been easy to be on the straight and narrow when we lived in the same apartment complex but now almost impossible—at least that's how I felt—to continue Bible study. So what did I do? The only thing I was comfortable with—my life of sin. Oh, I could tell you hundreds of sad, sick stories of which now plague my emotions and tear me up, but I won't.

I'm going to skip seven years later when I was working in a psych nursing home, hating my job where they treated the employees like no better than slaves, but they paid well. So, one day at work, I went to a patient's room to administer his insulin and saw that he wasn't in his room. The bathroom door was closed so I opened it and the patient grabbed me by the neck as he was falling to the ground. I quickly swung around so that we would fall on his bed instead of the floor and he landed on top of me. As I slowly moved out from under him, my body felt like it 'literally' came apart. Every joint and every muscle felt like a jolt of lightning hit. I saw stars—black with white dots—and I knew I was hurt. The patient, I learned later, had a low sugar level and after given his dose of insulin, was all right. I, on the other hand, went straight to the ER and was sent home with a script for an anti-inflammatory medication. The medication did nothing for me. I began physical therapy a couple of days later where the doctors there told me that a trauma like that subjected me to instant arthritis, carpal tunnel syndrome, and a host of other problems. Physical therapy only lasted six weeks and after that I was on my own. Just to walk was so difficult. My knees hurt so badly and I felt like all my joints were out of place. I wasn't even able to pick up a fork and hold onto it. I lost weight. By this time I was prescribed Vicodin for the pain, which really didn't do much to help. For weeks I couldn't think about anything as I was consumed with pain. I remember thinking and praying out loud, "Please God take me out of this pain—just take me."

At this time Joey, now called Joe, was seeing this girl who actually looked like Satan but I felt helpless against all the forces around me. I had been out of work for three months now due to my injuries and remember this one night very clearly. It was right after the New Year and I had gotten myself into my bed writhing in pain and, just to put it plainly, I gave up. I remember slowly drifting out of the pain into a slow-motion image of a broken down bridge I was trying to cross holding onto the old rope railings. Above me was a brand new bridge with beams of gold. I remember the broken bridge crumbling beneath my feet and as I began to panic, reaching up really high to grab onto the bottom of the new shiny golden bridge above me, holding tightly as the bridge below me fell. From out of nowhere—or everywhere—a calm, loving, nurturing voice said, 'Change Ahab'. At that moment my entire body and soul shuttered as I realized that this was God—talking to me! In a split second, my life flashed before me and a total sense of shame, humility, and awe came over me. GOD SPOKE TO ME—me—a low-life drunk and drug addict whose existence equaled to less than a piece of dirt. How or why would our God even waste time thinking about me, much less talk to me? I was more than overwhelmed—I was transformed! In a matter of a minute, a split second in time, I not only realized who I had become and demoralized myself, but felt a true forgiveness and realized that it was God I had been seeking my entire life. He was not only real, but alive. God is real and talked to me! There was not an ounce of self-doubt that this was real.

I woke up a new person—a different person—one with no doubts—no fears—no demons—I felt clear inside. I was shaking all over, inside and outside. Everything that had torn my spirit to shreds was gone—my demons were gone—my hope was restored—I wanted to shout from the rooftop to tell everyone about God. Oh, and I did! I got up, made my bed and called work and told them that I would be in that day. I went back to work that same day and told my story to everyone. They felt the truth coming from God's spirit inside me. There was no hiding it. In an instant my life changed— forever. My addictions of drugs, cigarettes and alcohol were completely gone. Of course, the reality of it was that I had burned some bridges behind me that had to be rebuilt and it took some time to mend those bridges and even now, 14 years later, the hurt that I had caused still remains but I am on a different plane now and have a completely open view of things that I couldn't see before.

I see things differently now and have this sense of knowledge that could only come from God. I can look at people and feel who they are inside and know their intentions. Cigarettes, drugs, and alcohol were taken away in that split second of time. I wasn't me any longer—I was God's. I began reading the Bible and the more I read, the more knowledge God gave me; it was almost as if the words in the Bible became brighter and when that happened, a feeling of peace came over me. Instantly I understood those words. Sometimes God gave me two or three different interpretations and I understood each one and how it related to today.

This was all too amazing to keep to myself. I continued to tell everyone about everything I was learning and of my entire story. Over the last 14 years, I learned of a few people that were called by God, too, but they ignored Him. A true sadness came over me when they told me this story. This was one of the reasons why I decided to put my story into print. Of course, I called Bob to tell him the good news and we still keep in touch to this day.

Well, you read about my life 'before' God—so I would like to tell you about this new life God has blessed me with. You already know why I didn't think I deserved it but choose me He did. I now have joy in my life that I didn't have before; I now take responsibility for my actions as I know I have to answer to Him. I have hope now—where I had none before—and faith has been restored in me that I can now remember having as a very young child. I don't claim any of this of my own doing. If you remember what I said about my previous life, I was lost inside myself and wasn't able to change any of it.

Everything changed for me—the way I saw people and situations and my approach to all of it. I immediately reached out to my family and tried to open their eyes to what I was now seeing. I know that they were happy for me but after a time I realized that these things that I was learning were for my eyes only and we are each reached by God in His way—not mine—and in His time, not mine. But still, it didn't stop me from telling the world how I see things.

Over the past 14 years, a relationship has formed between Jesus and myself. He has performed so many miracles and given me so many favors that I still get 'goosebumps' when I know that He is doing this or has done that. One of the bigger miracles that comes to mind is the night I was driving home on I-95 from New York after a visit with my daughter. It was about 3 AM—I enjoy driving at night since there is not much traffic. So, I'm going about 70 miles an hour and I see some flashing lights way up ahead. I could tell that it was not the police or an emergency vehicle as the lights were different. Then, all of a sudden, I look to the right side of the road and in a moment, everything began to go in slow-motion. There was a car pulled off the road and a man standing at the side of it. I saw his face and it appeared to have a horrified look on it and he was looking right at me. My stomach dropped and I knew there was something terribly wrong. As I slowly turned my head toward the road, right in front of me was this log, and at the same time I saw the log, I saw the truck with the flashing lights carrying logs which had a broken chain where the logs had come loose. This all happened in a split second—the man looking horrified—the log—the truck. Immediately I felt a piercing fear—this was it—I'm going to die. It was too late to break or turn and so I resigned myself to a fate of death. All of a sudden I felt a 'thud, thud'—as if I just ran over a branch. I looked over at the truck driver's amazed look at me and went on. I could not believe what just happened. I slowed down in order to absorb it all. I look back through my rear-view mirror and cried. I bawled and as I was bawling, I thanked God for what he just took me through. It all just felt like a dream, but it wasn't.

And I'll tell you this—my life changed greatly after God called me Ahab. I told you I began reading the Bible and after about six months, I learned that Ahab married Jezebel and happened to be the worst king of Israel. That's who God compared me to—the worst king of Israel. I felt ashamed of myself when I realized this and cried. Boy, God sure knows how to pack a punch. Over the next few years, I began to settle into a new life—one like I've never known. It took me a while but I slowly began to care about myself. My health became important—spiritual and physical. God became first in my life. I learned in 1st John that God wants us to confess our sins to him and repent for them and that when we do that he forgives not only that sin but all of our sins. When I learned that, I realized that the only way to be in God's light all of the time was to practice that act of righteousness every time I sinned. So, I repent for my sins many times during the day being on God's 'watchtower' and take every thought captive to see if it was a sin or not. That took quite a while to accomplish as my mind used to go a hundred miles an hour. I began to realize that God had given me a second chance but that I had to work to keep it. So, now with my newly found money (that I no longer needed for drugs, cigarettes, or alcohol), I had gotten myself a one-bedroom apartment in a moderately classed apartment complex with a pool and an exercise room.

By this time, my daughter Linda was married for the second time and had four children. She still lived in Long Island. My second child Christine graduated from Columbia College and moved to California. She had gotten involved with professional cycling and put her own team together. Steve had gotten married and moved to Pennsylvania and allowed himself to separate from all of his family. Joe stayed with that girl and also allowed himself to be separated from all of his family. I knew where Joe worked at the time and I would go there when he got off from work just to keep them 'in the loop' about the family. Joe finally ended up leaving her.

So, about a year after I moved into this apartment, my brother called and wanted to know about Florida. He was leaving his ex-wife and was thinking about moving with his son. At the time he was living with his 14-year-old son and his ex-wife who was addicted to drugs. I felt his need to take his son away from all that, so I invited him to stay with me for a few weeks. If he liked it, he could go from there. He took me up on it and arrived later in a beat-up old van that got him and his son from New Jersey to Florida and my apartment. My brother and I had a volatile relationship on and off but all was forgotten when he got here. They stayed for about two months until they got their own place. I could sense that their relationship was far from a loving one. It was really good to see him though. I hadn't seen him for over 10 years.

So, I went to work every day, came home, and on my two days off, I shopped. I had become so used to not having any friends that it became a way of life, my life. I guess you don't really miss something you've never had. I was a hermit—I had my computer and my Bible and that was all I needed at that time. I couldn't wait to get home from work to see what God was going to teach me that night. I stayed in that apartment for about four years until I got a call from Bob. He wanted me to move in with him to help with his expenses. Well, I ended up staying there for just over a year. I had applied for a mortgage to buy this adorable home in St. Petersburg which had three bedrooms and a mother-in-law apartment. I just fell in love with this home. It was built just one year after my birth and was a cinderblock home with two big oaks in the front yard which protected the hot Florida sun from beating on the roof. It had so many windows that I almost felt like I was outside. It had that country look which I always loved. Well, I got the house and moved in and I'm still there to this day.

I have a wonderful neighbor Mel who in his own time, after I moved in, worked in the mother-in-law apartment after coming home from his regular job, to get it tenant ready. He gave me his time for free and I paid for materials. He finally finished it off after 3 years and it was beautiful. It was on the small side but had its own kitchen and bathroom and was ready to rent. The apartment had its own entrance on the side of the house with a sliding glass door, its own patio, and a privacy fence that Joe had put up for me around the house. I have a long, wide driveway and even had a parking space picked out for the person who would rent the apartment.

My life had begun to be so blessed in so many ways that I can't even begin to tell you. God conquered my addictions but I also acquired a sense of peace in my life. I was able to read the Bible for a few hours without being distracted. I could watch a television show for a full hour without having to get up and down every few minutes due to the anxiety that I had been suffering. I could concentrate without these fleeting thoughts coming into my head constantly. It was amazing—I wasn't 'in trouble' anymore.

It still took a lot of work to begin to rebuild my relationships with my children. There was so much guilt I was still dealing with but I learned over the years that guilt, in itself, is a sin, and knowing this I finally learned how to forgive myself. You know the old saying, 'you made your bed—now sleep in it', really hit home with me. All at once my eyes were open and there was no way to shut them. With no drinking or drugs, there was no way 'out' anymore—I had to face it all. One would think that God gave me 'new' life so everything would be okay now. Wrong! It didn't work that way. He wants to know that I want to keep this new life, enough to suffer for it. I stepped up for Him as I knew there was no doubt I wanted to keep Him in my life. There was no going back for me. So, I still suffer backlashes from people regarding my 'old' life from those who still have not forgiven me. The thing that gives me solace is the knowledge that God puts each one of us through what He knows will bring us back to Him. This is all God's plan for each one of us. I was born into my family and went through what was necessary to get me to where I am today. Each one of us is on a different path which leads us back to God. God is our Creator and only He knows what is best for us.

You remember the 'dream' that was given to me about my brother Christopher? Well, I cannot even begin to tell you how many of those 'dreams' were given to me in my new life. I have seen Christopher many times since, and have also seen my parents, Patty Ann, and my brother Tom, as he had passed away four years after he arrived in Florida. His son found him after he hadn't seen him for two days laying in his bed—dead. I have even seen myself not only in heaven but also as an older lady in a wheelchair here on earth.

These dreams began after I moved into my home. Now, every time I experience one of these dreams, I know that my 'body' is in bed but it feels natural to be in another place. At the time I don't question where I am; I just accept it.

There was this one long dream which may have preceded the others, but I'm not sure. I 'woke up' getting out of a convertible pulled off to the side of the highway. Linda, my son Steve, and Christine were with me. They were hungry and I had noticed at the top of this mountain they were selling Chinese food. I knew what they wanted to eat and began to climb this rickety wooden bridge with rope railings. The floor of the bridge was made up of separate pieces of wood and the bridge swayed as I walked. I looked back and saw Linda and Steve but Christine was gone. I also saw my horse which was on a rope attached to the back of my car. It was a black-and-white pinto whose name I have now forgotten (but I knew it in the dream). So, I get up to the top, get the food, and bring it down to the kids. It cost something like $52. Linda said, "You paid too much. That's not worth it. Go back and get your money," so I went back up the bridge and told him that they overcharged me. They told me I have to get my money back 'up there' as they pointed to a higher point. So I went out further and was shuffled onto a 'zip line'. As it was moving over the crowd, I was pulling my shorts down as I didn't want anyone to see my private area. This line seat had pulled my shorts way up to an uncomfortable position. During this ride, I noticed that the 'zip line' was going around the San Francisco Bay—where Christine had lived. I was very self-conscious as it moved. It headed into a tunnel which was over the water and I remember I was so scared that I would hit into the sides of the tunnel. I came out of the tunnel and saw the rocks on the side of the mountain along the path of the 'zip line'. The ride got back to the beginning where Linda and Steve were waiting. It slowed down but I couldn't maneuver my body out of the seat in time to get off. Steve was upset as he yelled, "Mom, just jump off!"

But Linda tried to comfort him and said, "Mom is older now and can't move like that." So, now I'm going around for the second time. I'm still self-conscious about how people see me but not as much. I went through the tunnel again but this time less afraid, and now coming out of the tunnel, I noticed some green plants or trees growing on the side of the mountain whereas before the mountain looked like slates of rock, cold, and scary.

I came to the end of the ride again for the second time and as it slowed down I again tried to get off, but didn't try as hard. Linda yelled to me, "I'll be in the white house over there!" I looked over and saw the house that she was talking about and felt it was alright. Now, this was my third time around, but this time I wasn't holding on tight. I felt totally relaxed and began to look around. Everything looked beautiful. As I noticed the tunnel coming up, it began to look alive. I noticed the stones that the bridge was made out of and it was as if each stone had a life of its own and moved as if they were all one. I was overcome with joy and excitement and even swayed the zip line as I approached the tunnel. The tunnel swayed to my movement and it was as if the tunnel and I were a part of each other. When I got out of the tunnel this time, I saw that the trees and plants and flowers on this side of the mountain were all alive and singing to me 'This is where the Lord is taking you' over and over and over. The voices that were singing had to be the voices of angels. I awoke with such joy and overwhelmed with a feeling of peace and love knowing that the Lord had talked to me again. This time through angels. There was not a bit of doubt in my heart. In this dream I realized the more I worried about this world, my appearance, and my children, the less I saw God's beauty. In the moment that I stopped worrying, everything reversed.

So, after being in my new home for a year, my job was becoming very stressful. I had lost a lot of weight and finally when I got pushed too far, I quit. The thing was, though, I had no other job waiting for me. I did find another job—part-time—which worked itself into full-time. I was there for about a year and a half and this job became as horrible as the last one. I had 36 patients to care for, medication administration, and wound care—not to mention the paperwork for new admissions. Then, one day, the four shift nurses (me being one of them), were called to the DON's (Director of Nursing) office. We were told that she had hired an RN to do all the admissions and all the wound care from now on. Now this was a big deal. If you know anything about nursing, you would know this would be a great timesaver. Well, I was ecstatic and even went back in the office to thank her. Well, that very next day, I got a new admission who happened to have a very large wound. All shift long, this new RN repeatedly told me, "I got this. Don't worry," so I believed that she would carry out her job and do the admission and take care of his wound. I went home and never even gave it another thought. The next day when I arrived at work, I was called into the director of nursing office. She told me that she had to let me go since I didn't do the admission or the wound care. I was astounded when she was saying this, "You hired an RN for that very

73

same job." I answered. Her response was, "Whose patient was he?" At that point I knew that no matter what I said, it wouldn't matter. Someone was going to be responsible and I knew it wouldn't be her. So I walked out.

I was living paycheck to paycheck throughout my life, so not having a job was a big deal to me. My bills now became late and I had gotten a foreclosure letter for my home after 3 months of not having an income. I looked and looked for another job.

I never had anyone to turn to in my life, so it was just me to face this crisis. At that time my son, Joe, had moved in with me and one day, as he walked out of his room, he said, "What are we going to do, Mom?"

Without hesitation, I answered, "You know, Joe, I talk about God a lot, but this time I'm going to let him handle it. If He wants us to live in the street, we will, and if His wishes are for us to be hungry, we'll be hungry. I give it all to you Lord, in the name of Jesus." And as I said that, a sense of calm came over me and immediately all the worrying was gone.

So, let me tell you what the Lord did for me in the next three weeks. I had just turned 66-years-old and so I called up Social Security to apply for benefits. The woman I spoke to asked me if I had ever been married before and if the marriage had lasted more than 10 years. I told her yes. Well, this woman took the time to tell me that I was able to collect Social Security from one of them and in turn, my own Social Security would be able to grow until the age of 70. There was only a difference of $200 a month between mine and his, so I opted for his. I never even knew I was qualified for this. She said I would get my first check in two weeks. Secondly, my neighbor finished the mother-in-law apartment that week and I got it rented out right away. And thirdly, as I was scouring the Internet searching for a job—not in nursing this time as I was 'done' with nursing, this Hospice employment ad literally drops onto the computer screen. I even jumped back as that happened. I thought to myself, *Hospice would never hire someone like me.* I was prompted to fill out the application and send my resume with it, which I did. I didn't think about it again until three days later when I received an email from Hospice requesting me to come in for an interview. I was shocked. Never in my wildest dreams would I think I could be hired as a Hospice nurse. The title on the application said 'Continuous Care LPN'. I didn't quite know what that meant but was about to find out. So, I went in and took a couple of tests and I was hired on the spot. I still had no idea just what I got hired as. It turns out that the three-week training started the beginning of the next week and it was 'paid training'. WHAT?? I was in shock—within three weeks—got my first Social Security check, rent from the mother-in-law apartment, and a job that I had secretly hoped for my entire career as a nurse. Continuous care, as I discovered during my training, was giving last hour nursing care to dying patients. I was to have one patient who had less than five days to live and care for them and the grieving family—and they were going to pay me for this! God is good! God is great!! And so began my new career as a hospice nurse, Social Security recipient with Medicare benefits, and a landlord, all of which I still am to this day. There was no doubt in my mind that it was all the Lord's doing.

Remember the 'dream' I had with my brother Christopher? So, since God called me back, I have had so many dreams about my family that I can't even remember how many. My brother Tom died in 2012 and he had never believed in God and used to tease me about 'my' God. So, one night, that same year he died, I saw him with Christopher. They both looked the same age—probably young 30s. My brother Tom, in the dream, gave me this look, like 'Sorry I was wrong—I didn't know'. But they both looked so happy.

By this time, during my 'dreams', I knew that I was somewhere else and that my physical body was in bed as I had so many of these occurrences already. So, one night, I woke up in this bright—but not the bright that hurts your eyes—space and heard the light-hearted giggling of little girls. I looked over and saw maybe six or seven little girls playing next to some sort of counter. They appeared to be about 7 years old and were laughing and giggling like little girls do. Out of the corner of my right eye, I saw this girl moving over toward the counter. She was just moving, not walking or running. The second I saw her, I thought to myself, *That looks like Patty Ann*. The second I thought that—she was inches from my face holding these little glasses with no rims and said, "So that's what you look like," and suddenly she was back with the other children. God had showed me that this was indeed Patty Ann, as when she was in this world with me—her eyes were unable to focus as they would move from side to side. "I saw my baby. She was happy and could move and communicate."

Another time, I woke up in a room or in a small apartment and my grandmother leaned over at the doorway and as I saw her, I said, "Hi, Grandma." I wasn't surprised at all to see her—it was all just as a matter of fact.

She said, "You know you're going to move, don't you?"

I answered, "No, Grandma, where am I moving to?"

"Up North," she answered. "You're moving up North, so get your house in order."

Cheerfully I answered, "Okay, I will."

So when I woke up that day I realized that 'North' was heaven as I pictured a map on the wall—North is up. This actually gave me a real sense of peace. I felt no fear or anxiety—just peace.

Another time, I saw myself in heaven. I felt amazement as I looked at myself and remembered thinking—that's me— you are me! I had silvery-white short hair and wearing what reminded me of a gown—a white gown—not a wedding gown but just a flowing gown. That one really made me think, but I guess since there is no time in heaven, I can understand it. I also had another vision of myself apparently in this world, as

76

I was sitting in a wheelchair. I looked to be about 96 years old and where I got that number I don't know. It looked like a family picture where there were a few tall men standing around me and some other people who I really didn't look at because I was really concentrating on the woman in the wheelchair. Once I realized it was me—the vision went away. Now, I don't know what that means—will I live to be that age? I don't know.

There was another dream I had of this young Egyptian boy with beautiful black hair, pulled back into a ponytail braid, and bronze skin. When I took a good look at him, I felt (or knew) it was Christopher. Even during this dream I was aware that Christopher looked different, although in my heart I knew it was Christopher. Wow! This opened the possibility of 'maybe there is reincarnation', who knows. Maybe we keep coming back to this life until we get it right? With God, everything is possible. Maybe I was Ahab and the worst king of Israel? If that is true—look at where I am now. I don't know where this life will take me, but at least now I know there is Someone who loves me and has forgiven me for the things I've done and who will accept me just the way I am.

Another experience that I had was on my job in a nursing home. I had visited a patient named Patricia who was imminent and it was reported to me that she hadn't talked for days now. She was the only patient in the room and I was the only visitor that she had at that time. As I sat at her bedside, I saw that she was looking up at the ceiling, which is common with patients who are close to death. Then she turned to me and said, "Who are all those children?"

This really startled me, as I was told that she had not talked for a while. I answered her, as this was all too common to me, "They have come to see you."

Working as a Hospice nurse, I witness many, many spiritual encounters that the patients have, so I just assumed that she was seeing angels. She looked up again at the ceiling and said something like, "Oh."

She turned to me once more and said, "Now there are three Patricia's in the room."

When she said three Patricia's, I immediately felt my daughter's presence. I didn't answer her because I was in shock. She turned again to the ceiling and said, "Okay," and immediately turned around to me and asked, "Who's Joe?"

Now by this time I knew that my daughter Patty Ann was talking to this woman. I answered with a very shaky voice in a low tone, "That's my son." I just couldn't believe what was happening.

Looking at the ceiling again she made something of an "Ewwww" sound and looked at me very seriously and said, "Does he smoke?"

At this point I couldn't say a word since I knew it was Patty Ann talking to this woman. I was stunned. Again she looked up at the ceiling and made a sound of relief (like a sigh), turned to me and said, "Of course he doesn't smoke—he's only 2 ½ years old," (which was the age of Patty Ann when she passed).

This was the first time that Patty Ann had spoken to me through someone else. There was another occasion months later, in a different nursing home, when a CNA came to me and asked, "Is your name Patty Ann?"
    I was in a room with the patient when the CNA came into the room. I had never met this woman before and this CNA wasn't even assigned to this patient.

I answered her very humbly, "No, but I had a daughter named Patty Ann who passed."

She said, "I knew that, as she has been talking to me about you. I could sense that you were the type of person who would understand and not be scared. I have spirits come to me all the time and have for years. Patty Ann tells me that she is with you all the time and that when you walk into a room and forget what you went there for, she is the one to remind you. She wanted me to give you the message that she is with you all the time and she knows it would give you a lot of comfort knowing this."

I was so touched that day. God is so good that he sent a second person as a witness that this was definitely Patty Ann. I feel so blessed. So, so blessed.

So, presently I am a full time hospice nurse and absolutely love my job. I still own the same home, the mother-in-law apartment still brings me an income, and I am now collecting my own Social Security which at the age of 70 for me is $600 a month more than if I would have begun collecting it at age 66. And to top it off, I have a 401(k) plan where 25% of my income goes every month, which will be my retirement money to fall back on that I had never even thought of doing before.

I still have a hard time forgiving myself for the past, especially for the heartbreak that I put my children through. God has given me so much and has made my life worth living for, with Him right here with me, but I guess that He really wants me to learn from all this. He has taken away from me the prison that I was in with my drinking and drugs, taken away my anxieties and fears and has given me such an ease in life that I didn't even know existed.

I have always believed in God even with everything that I have experienced in my life. I have never blamed God or even thought about blaming Him. There was a short time during my adolescent years that for some reason I began to go to Mass before school every Wednesday and Friday. At that time I felt really close to God and used to picture what Heaven would be like. I remember when Christopher was in second grade, at the age of seven, and had a friend named John O'Connor. This boy knew he was going to die—he had cancer. One night when his parents were tucking him in, he said, "Tonight's the night,"—he knew. The family had come over and told my parents the next day. This may have been the catalyst that had begun my journey toward God. We never know throughout our lives who is put into our path or what circumstances we have to endure. At the time some things may seem overbearing, but what I can tell you is that if you have an open heart and don't lose it to the sorrows of the world—God is there—He is here—He is alive—He is real—He Is. Trusting is believing without seeing.